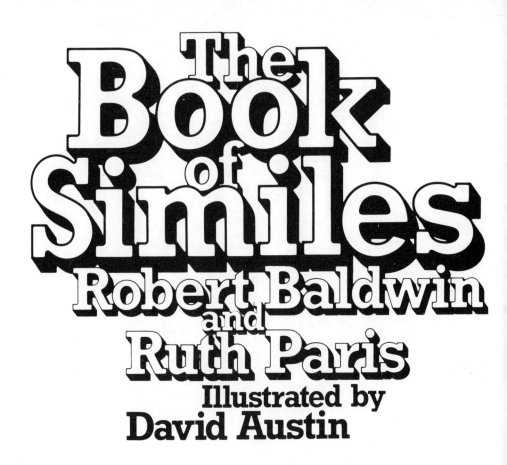

The Book of Similes

Robert Baldwin and Ruth Paris

Illustrated by David Austin

Routledge & Kegan Paul

London, Boston, Melbourne and Henley

First published in 1982
by Routledge & Kegan Paul Ltd
39 Store Street, London WC1E 7DD,
9 Park Street, Boston, Mass. 02108, USA,
Broadway House, Newtown Road,
Henley-on-Thames, Oxon RG9 1EN and
296 Beaconsfield Parade, Middle Park,
Melbourne, 3206, Australia and
Phototypeset by Input Typesetting Ltd, London
and printed in Great Britain by
T.J. Press (Padstow) Ltd,
Padstow, Cornwall

ISBN 0–7100–9285–7
ISBN 0–7100–9456–6 (Pbk)

To Felicity and David

Acknowledgments

The first debt of those compiling a parasitical book must be to all those, the anonymous and the named, whose works have been plundered in the search for material. This we gratefully acknowledge.

In particular we thank the following for their helpful responses to our request for similes: Kingsley Amis; Jilly Cooper; Ray Galton; Cliff Hanley; Denis Healey; Adrian Henri; Patrick Moore; Frank Muir; Denis Norden; Michael Parkinson; Alan Simpson; Leslie Thomas and Terry Wogan.

We are also grateful to Roger McGough and Victoria Wood for their permission to use lines from their work and to Mark Findlay for supplying many of the antipodean phrases.

Preface

The idea for this book came from Scottish football
commentators, who, for many years now have
enlivened each match report with at least one
description of stunning incongruity ('Partick Thistle
took the field today like Boadicea out to take on the
Romans'). As well as saying something about Scottish
football, this practice raised the question of where
such expressions come from. It seemed that, in the
absence of any reference book, journalists were
resorting to invention.

We hope with this volume to fill the gap by offering
a collection of similes and expressions of comparison
to suit various occasions. It is essentially a light-
hearted and arbitrary selection: for a more scholarly
and systematic compilation see F. Wilstack's *Dictionary
of Similes*, Harrap, 1917.

The book is laid out according to key words. These
have either been supplied by the named author or
have been taken as implied and inserted by us. We
apologise for any ensuing misinterpretation.

When dealing with phrases in common usage, as
many of these are, it is not always possible properly
to attribute them to the original author. We therefore
apologise for any wrongly attributed phrases, and will
endeavour to make corrections in any future edition.

On the proper use of similes, one of their major
exponents, Raymond Chandler, commented that one
should concentrate on whatever is being described
rather than divert attention to the vehicle of
comparison. He criticised a Ross Macdonald simile
('the seconds piled up precariously like a pile of poker
chips') for erring in this way. We have used no such
discretion and no doubt Chandler would have
objected to many of the similes we have included.

At the time of writing, the effect of providing a
reference book of this kind is hard to assess. We will

know that progress has been made when, some time
in the future, a footballer lies writhing on the
ground and we hear on the commentary 'Keegan is
moaning like a she-sheldrake when its mate has had
the tip of its wing hurt by a hawk!'

The Similes

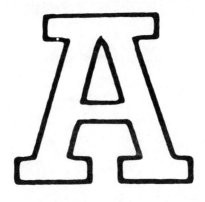

Abandon	. . . the reckless abandon of a night watchman with arthritis. *Raymond Chandler*
Abruptness	of a cork leaving a champagne bottle. *P. G. Wodehouse*
Acid	as a load of unripe grapefruit. *Richard Gordon*
Actor	. . . like a cigar; the more you puff him, the smaller he gets. *Anon.*
Admirable	about as admirable as the droppings of hippopotami. *Norman Mailer*
Admiration	the same kind of admiration one would feel for a streaker at Queen Victoria's funeral. *William F. Buckley*
Adonis	. . . looks as if he was made out of ivory and rose-leaves. *Oscar Wilde*
Advertising	Doing business without advertising is like winking at a girl in the dark; you know what you are doing, but nobody else does. *Anon.*
Advertising	. . . the rattling of a stick inside a swill bucket. *George Orwell*

Advice	. . . pieces of advice . . . stick to your teeth like soft caramels. *Jean-Paul Sartre*

3

Aeroplane	The aeroplane sat on the tarmac like a man with his arms in plaster. *Alida Baxter*
Affable	as a wet dog. *Alfred Henry Lewis*
Afro hairstyle	like an enormous black dandelion in seed, blown, all its soft spindles standing out. *Saul Bellow*
Afternoon	buzzes like lazy bees. *Dorothy Parker*
Age	She is rotting quietly under her skirts with a melancholy smile, like the smell of violets which is sometimes given off by decomposing bodies. *Jean-Paul Sartre*
Aggrieved	like a bulldog which has just been kicked in the ribs and had its dinner sneaked by the cat. *P. G. Wodehouse*
Agile	makes a conger eel look arthritic. *Anon.*
Agitated	I agitated them like a hot poker in a mug of claret. *Peter de Vries*
Agitated	for the next thirty seconds cats on hot bricks could have picked up tips from me. *P. G. Wodehouse*
Alarmed	He felt like George Washington owning up about the cherry tree and then finding his dad after him with the axe. *Richard Gordon*
Ale	imbued with a most delicious creaminess, as if a black cow had browsed all winter among malt in a kiln. *George Mackay Brown*
Ale	flowed like a leak in the Pacific. *Les Dawson*
Alert	as an eel. *Anon. (Scots)*
Alert	as a radar specialist. *Alistair Cooke*
Alimony	Paying alimony is like feeding hay to a dead horse. *Groucho Marx*
All over the place	like a mad-woman's knitting/custard/lunch-box. *Anon.*
Alligator	looked like a handbag filled with harmonicas. *Richard Brautigan*

Alluring	as a bus driver's sock.	*Victoria Wood*
Alone	like a shag on a rock.	*Anon.*
Aloof	like you was Lady Nevershit.	*Arnold Wesker*
American	as the suction-cupped flag.	*Ken Kesey*

American	as a sawed-off shotgun.	*Dorothy Parker*
American politics	The political alternatives in America now are like putting Band-Aid on cancer.	*Shirley Maclaine*
Americans	are like a rich father who wishes he knew how to give his sons the hardships that made him rich.	*Robert Frost*
Amiable	. . . the amiable impersonality of the pub dog who has been patted too often – still polite, but longing for closing time.	*Jilly Cooper of Robert Redford*
Amount	enough to choke a boa constrictor.	*Anon.*
Andrews (Julie)	Working with her is like being hit over the head with a Valentine card.	*Christopher Plummer*
Angelic	as barbed wire.	*Patrick Campbell*
Angry	exhibiting all the symptoms of rabies.	*Anon.*
Angry	simmering like a corked volcano.	*Anon.*
Angry	he danced slightly, like a ferret on fire.	*William McIlvanney*

Angry	like a cinnamon bear with its foot in a trap. *P. G. Wodehouse*
Annoyed	as a cock maggot in a sink-hole. *Anon.*
Anonymous	as a nickel in a parking meter. *Raymond Chandler*
Apologetic	looking like a spaniel dog that's just made a mess on the mat. *Gerald Kersh*
Appeal	all the winsome appeal of a clockwork boil. *Alan Coren*
Appearance	look like a sink full of unwashed dishes. *Anon.*
Appearance	look like the Wreck of the Hesperus. *P. G. Wodehouse*
Appetising	as a glass and a half of cold pork fat. *Clive James*
Appetite	like an anorexic sparrow. *Anon.*
Appetite	like a waste disposal unit. *Anon.*
Apprehensive	like a Reverend Abbess receiving two rather leprous mendicants. *Sir Arthur Conan Doyle*
Apprehensive	with the expression of the Prodigal Son having just rung the doorbell. *Richard Gordon*
Architecture	In style it managed to combine elements of both East and West . . . it looked as though Windsor Castle had been used for the artificial insemination of Brighton Pavilion. *Tom Sharpe*

Arm	like trying to dig your fingers into the inflated tyre of a five ton truck. *Gerald Kersh*

Art	is like a border of flowers along the course of civilisation. *Lincoln Stephens*
Assurance	of a woman who has swam the Channel against a rip tide. *Tallulah Bankhead*
At home	as much at home as a Pierre Cardin shirt in a pile of sale seconds. *Mike Aitken*
At home	like astigmatism, I made myself at home. *Richard Brautigan*
Audience	sparkled like a city seen at night from an airplane. *Anon.*
Audience	Audiences, like salad dressings, are never the same twice. *Robert Morley*
Austere	as a tree full of owls. *Anon.*
Author	An author who speaks about his own books is almost as bad as a mother who talks about her own children. *Benjamin Disraeli*
Autogyro	looks like a high-heeled dodgem speared by a rotary clothes line. *Clive James*
Awaken	He twitched erect like a puppet. *William McIlvanney*
Awkward	as a blind dog in a meat shop. *Anon.*
Awkward	as a cow on ice. *Anon.*

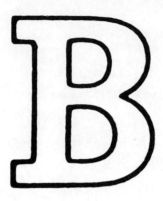

Baby	looked like a homicidal poached egg. *P. G. Wodehouse*
Bacall (Lauren)	as seductive as Eve, as cool as the serpent. *Louise Brooks*
Bag	one of those awkward looking square bags that makes you think of a sister of mercy taking first aid to the wounded. *Raymond Chandler*
Baggy	a coat baggy enough to take in lodgers. *William McIlvanney*
Bainbridge (Beryl)	I do look somewhat gaunt – not unlike that grim soul on the old poster 'Keep Death off the Road'. *Beryl Bainbridge*
Bald	. . . a few hairs spread carefully over his head like fiddle strings. *J. M. Barrie*
Bald	as a grapefruit. *Raymond Chandler*
Bald	with a few strands of hair combed across his head, like anchovies across a boiled egg. *Jilly Cooper*
Bald	as a cue ball. *Ed McBain*
Bald	as some lunar sea of senility. *Albert Morris*
Bare	as the behind of a bürgermeister's baby. *Anon.*
Barge	laying like a tethered hippo. *Leslie Thomas*
Barrymore (John)	moved through a movie scene like an exquisite paper knife. *Heywood Broun*
Beard	like he was peeking over a hedge. *Anon.*

8

Beard	like a quickset hedge.	*G. MacDonald Fraser*
Bearded	like the pard.	*William Shakespeare*
Beauty	Elke Sommer was a dried up old prune in comparison.	*S. J. Perelman*
Bed	looked like a ping-pong table without the flexibility.	*Clive James*
Bedraggled	like something the cat brings in of a wet night.	*Anon.*
Beech Trees	. . . are feathered orange like buff-orpington hens.	*D. H. Lawrence*
Benign	like a vicar at a prizegiving.	*Anon.*
Bent	as a boomerang.	*Anon.*
Bent	As a nine-bob note.	*Anon.*
Bent	as an electric golf-club.	*Gordon Williams*
Berserk	like a windmill gone to the bad.	*Anon. (Ozark – USA)*
Betrayed	I knew how a Brooklyn Dodger fan must have felt on hearing that his favourite pitcher had defected to the Chicago White Sox.	*David Niven*
Better	than a poke in the eye with a burnt stick.	*Anon.*

Better	than a slap in the belly with a wet fish. *Anon.*
Big	He was built like a Russian war memorial. *Gavin Lyall*
Biographer	So-and-so's dirty little fingers rifle through his subject's private life like a hick detective investigating a pimp's account book. *Martin Amis*
Birthmark	looked just like an old car parked on his head. *Richard Brautigan*
Black	as a kettle in hell. He was so black you'd have had to put a milk bottle on his head to find him in the dark. He looked a cross between a black angus calf and something fished out of the Mississippi on a moonless night. One tint darker and he would have disappeared altogether. *Nelson Algren*
Black	as crushed worms. *Anon.*
Black	as the Earl of Hell's riding boots/waistcoat. *Anon.*
Black	as wealth. *Saul Bellow*
Blackberry	jet as a blackcock's feather, sheened like the nose of a roe fawn. *David Stephen*
Blank expression	like a farm boy at a Latin lesson. *Raymond Chandler*
Blind	as a bank director. *Anon.*

Blinking	like a toad in a sand heap. *Anon.*
Bloated	as a squeezed cat. *Anon.*

Blonde	to make a bishop kick a hole in a stained glass window.	*Raymond Chandler*
Blubbering	like a seal.	*C. S. Calverley*
Blue	as the Angel Islington in Monopoly.	*Jilly Cooper*
Bluer	than a varicose vein in winter.	*Les Dawson*
Blush	like a black dog.	*Anon.*
Blush	like the back of a chimney.	*Anon.*
Boast	talks like he could put out hell with one bucket of water.	*Anon. (Ozark – USA)*
Boat	so lavishly outfitted it could have posed for the nautical den in Nelson Rockefeller's Fifth Avenue apartment.	*Hunter S. Thompson*
Bobbing	up and down like a duck in a mud-puddle.	*Anon.*
Bodies	as supple and as spare of fat as a conger eel's.	*Tom Davies*
Body	Her body streamed like a sonnet.	*Dorothy Parker*
Body	Her body against me like a bursting star.	*Peter de Vries*
Body	Her body seemed somehow to hang on her like somebody else's clothes.	*Peter de Vries*
Body	like a drawing by a student in a life class, who was sitting at the back without his specs.	*Victoria Wood*
Boil	a nose sore like a raspberry.	*Anthony Burgess*
Boisterous	as a Viking in drink.	*G. MacDonald Fraser*
Bore	make a fairy tale sound like a shopping list.	*William McIlvanney*
Bored	Evenings hung like seaweed around their necks.	*Dorothy Parker*
Borg (Bjorn)	Like a Volvo, Borg is rugged, has good after-sales service, and is very dull.	*Clive James*

Boring   as a pound of suet.   *Anon.*

Boring   as a boarding school on bath night.
                                              Dr Mervyn Stockwood

Bothered   as a toad in the sun.   *Raymond Chandler*

Bottom   like a little Michelangelo soaked in Brut. *Monty Python*

Bounce   like a pellet of quicksilver in a nervous man's palm.
                                              Dashiell Hammett

Boycott (Geoff) moved into the [Yorkshire] side like a cat stepping
                    into an armchair; spread himself with a century in
                    each of the Roses matches and settled into residence
                    for life.   *John Arlott*

Brain   like a cow's udder.   *Hunter S. Thompson*

Brain   like a large helping of fried noodles.   *Peter de Vries*

Brains   his brains rattle round like mustard seed in a rain
                    barrel.   *Anon. (USA)*

Brazen   as the seven gates of Thebes.   *Sue Arnold*

Break   like a bull through a cobweb.   *Anon. (Ozark – USA)*

Breasts   like two puppies fighting in a sack.   *Anon.*

Breasts   like two brioches, warm and steaming from the oven.
                                              Peter de Vries

Breath (lion's)   hot as oblivion, raw as blood.   *Saul Bellow*

Breath   like a badger's bum.   *Billy Connolly*

Breath   like a blowtorch.   *William McIlvanney*

Breathe   like an old Ford with a leaky head gasket.
                                                                  Raymond Chandler

Breed   like rats in a grain ship.   *Li Hung-Chang*

Breezy   as a Britisher coming in from a tiger hunt.
                                                                  Raymond Chandler

Bright   the people were as open and bright as a YMCA hut.
                                                                       John Buchan

Bristling   like a terrier spotting the postman.   *Richard Gordon*

British   as a hockey stick.   *Anon.*

British Army   overran our area like khaki diarrhoea.   *Alida Baxter*

Broke   as the Ten Commandments.   *Anon.*

Broke   as British Railways.   *Richard Gordon*

Brussels   Our car crawled into Brussels like an ant up an
                         unsavoury trouser leg.   *Alida Baxter*

Budget (March 1980) resembles nothing so much as the deliberations of a
                         corner shop grocer.   *Laurie Taylor*

Building	that looks like a dog-kennel or a Pepsi-Cola warehouse in St. Louis. *Hunter S. Thompson*
Bulging	like a deformity. *William McIlvanney*
Bulky	He was built the way one builds leather sofas, shiny and lumpy and with lots of solid stuffing. *Douglas Adams*
Bum	like a deftly closed tulip. *Leslie Thomas*
Bum	like frozen pastry after you've walked on it in stilettos. *Victoria Wood*
Burble	I can only burble like an old bird with its beak full of bias and soap. *Dylan Thomas*
Bush (Kate)	a hairstyle like an exploding armchair. *Clive James*
Busier	than a man with four hundred dollars and a thirst. *Damon Runyon*
Busy	as a one-legged man in a forest fire. *Anon.*
Busy	as a one-armed bill sticker in a gale. *Anon. (Australia)*
Busy	as ants at a picnic. *Anon. (Ozark – USA)*
Busy	as a buzz saw in a pine knot. *Anon. (Ozark – USA)*
Buzz	like a bee in a foxglove. *Anon.*

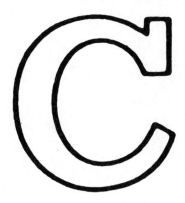

Calm	as a glacier.	*Anon.*
Calm	as a lake in heaven.	*W. S. Gilbert*
Calm	as a lizard on a sunny stone.	*Ken Kesey*
Camp	as a row of tents.	*Anon.*
Canada	has never been a melting pot; more like a tossed salad.	*Arnold Edinborough*
Canned Martini	tasted like brake fluid.	*Hunter S. Thompson*
Cantankerous	as a club-room of colonels.	*Alan Watkins*
Canteen pudding	Manchester Tart . . . a wedge-shaped piece of thickish, warm cardboard lightly smeared with raspberry flavoured red lead.	*Frank Muir*
Car	sounded as if it had the combustion engine's equivalent of asthma.	*William McIlvanney*
Car drivers	like K-registered lemmings.	*Richard Harris*
Care	with the exact care of a crack surgeon operating on a brain tumour.	*Raymond Chandler*
Careful	as porcupines making love.	*Anon.*
Carefully	as an out of work showgirl uses her last good pair of stockings.	*Raymond Chandler*
Careless	like the man looking for honey who overlooks the precipice.	*Anon. (Sanskrit)*

Caresses	broke upon me as the summer waves break upon Gibraltar. *Mark Twain*
Carpet	you could lose golf balls in. *Anon.*
Carpet	so soft it made me want to lie down and roll. *Raymond Chandler*
Carpet	the white carpet that went from wall to wall looked like a fresh fall of snow at Lake Arrowhead. *Raymond Chandler*
Carpet	so thick you could break your ankle in it. *Tom Wolfe*

Casual	as a young animal with Levi's on. *Richard Brautigan*
Cathedral	like Impressionism in stone. *Claude Monet*
Caution	with the caution of a pheasant hen returning to her nest. *Ross Macdonald*
Caution	his eyes took on a look of cautious reserve which you see in parrots when offered half a banana by a stranger of whose bona fides they are not convinced. *P. G. Wodehouse*
Caution	of one brushing flies off a sleeping Venus. *P. G. Wodehouse*

Cautious	as a camera-man engaged in shooting a family of fourteen lions. *Stella Gibbons*
Champagne	tasted like an apple peeled with a steel knife. *Aldous Huxley*
Chance	as much chance as a celluloid dog chasing an asbestos cat in hell. *Anon.*
Chance	as much chance as a fart in a hurricane. *Anon.*
Chance	as much chance as a one-legged man in an arse-kicking contest. *Anon.*
Chance	as much chance as a snowball in hell. *Anon.*
Chance	as much chance as a motorist's word against a policeman's. *New York Tribune*
Chance	as much chance as a one-armed blind man in a dark room trying to shove a pound of melted butter into a wildcat's left ear with a red hot needle. *P. G. Wodehouse*
Chaplin (Charlie)	when he found a voice to say what was on his mind, he was like a child of eight writing lyrics for Beethoven's Ninth. *Billy Wilder*
Character	as much character as a china shepherdess. *Anon.*
Charge	like a brain surgeon. *Saul Bellow*
Charity	is like molasses, sweet and cheap. *Anna Chapin Ray*
Charm	all the charm of a freshly boiled new potato. *Richard Gordon*
Charming	as a dead mouse in a loaf of bread. *Clive James*
Chatty	as a waxwork. *William McIlvanney*
Cheeks	flushed like a withered apple. *George Mackay Brown*
Cheeks	fat cheeks like twin rolls of smooth pink toilet paper. *Nathaniel West*

Cheery	just as cheery as if it were a winter morning on the high veld and we were off to ride down springbok. *John Buchan*
Chew gum	like a cow pulling its hoof out of mud. *Anon.*

Chin	like a wheelbarrow. *Gunter Grass*
Chin	like a wedge. *Dashiell Hammett*
Chins	folded into one another like the sections of a collapsible drinking cup. *Paul Gallico*
Chip	He carried a chip on each shoulder, like epaulettes. *Ross Macdonald*

Chipped	My sink's got more chips in it than a fish supper.
	Anon. (Glasgow)
Choice	like telling a man going to the electric chair that he has a choice of AC or DC. *Goodman Ace*
Choosey	as an alley cat. *Anon.*
Chuckle	like a sitting hen. *Victor Hugo*
Cicada	making this noise that sounds exactly like a very old pram, with squeaky, ovoid wheels, being pushed with unimaginable urgency uphill. *Patrick Campbell*
Cigarette	tasted like dung soaked in treacle. *G. MacDonald Fraser*
Cinema	may be described as a cross between a thought-saving machine and a cocktail. *John Galsworthy*
Circumstantial evidence	Some circumstantial evidence is very strong, as when you find a trout in the milk. *H. D. Thoreau*
Clâret	Château Fleet Street . . . the metallic flavour of this particular claret gives it a slight prison flavour as if the grape had been grown on the sunless side of Wormwood Scrubs. *John Mortimer*
Clean	as soap. *Anon.*
Clean	as a cat's ass. *Anon. (USA)*
Clean	as a hound's tooth. *Anon. (USA)*
Clean	an operating room clean as a Chevron station. *Richard Brautigan*
Cleaned out (cards)	I had been cleaned out like a spring chicken. *S. J. Perelman*
Cleanliness	'Cleanliness is Next to Godliness' – a sentiment about as logical as 'Lawn-mowing is Next to Madrigal-Singing'. *Frank Muir*
Clear	as the inside of a blackberry pie. *Anon.*
Clear	as tea room soup. *Groucho Marx*

Cleopatra	the body of a roll-top desk and the mind of a duck.
	Rowan Atkinson
Clever	as a box of monkeys. *Anon.*
Cling	like a damp dishcloth round a stove-pipe. *Anon.*
Clinging	like a barnacle to an Ethiopian battleship.
	Richard Brautigan
Clothes	He wears his clothes like a hide. *Samuel Butler*
Clothes	looked as if he put glue on his body and jumped through a wardrobe. *Peter MacDougall*
Clothes	The boilersuit looked as if it had been made for somebody else and he was just standing in.
	William McIlvanney

Clothes	stained like a collage of his past. *William McIlvanney*
Clothes	She wears her clothes as if they were thrown on with a pitchfork. *Jonathan Swift*
Clouds	lie over the chiming sky . . . like the dust-sheets over a piano. *Dylan Thomas*
Codpieces	the size of cabbages. *Tom Davies*
Coffee	tasting of dog fur. *Kingsley Amis*

Coffee   tasted like the socks of the Forgotten Man.
                                                            Raymond Chandler

Coffee pot   that smelled like sacks in a hot barn. *Raymond Chandler*

Cold   as an aunt's kiss.   *Anon.*

Cold   as a banker's heart.   *Anon.*

Cold   as Finnegan's feet the day they buried him.   *Anon.*

Cold   as the north side of a January gravestone by
                         moonlight.   *Anon.*

Cold   so cold even my goosepimples had goosepimples.
                                                                               Anon.

Cold   so cold I met a brass monkey on his way to the
                         welder's.   *Anon.*

Cold   as a well-digger's ass in the Klondike with a down
                         wind.   *Anon. (USA)*

Cold   as outer space.   *Saul Bellow*

Cold   as the ashes of love.   *Raymond Chandler*

Cold   as a frog.   *Anon.*

Cold   as a nightwatchman's feet.   *Raymond Chandler*

Cold   as a New England parson.   *Robert Coover*

Cold	cold enough to freeze a yak.	*Peter MacDougall*
Colder	than a barber's heart.	*Damon Runyon*
Colder	than a halibut on ice.	*P. G. Wodehouse*
Come-uppance	a case of the chickens coming home to roost, accompanied by three giant condors.	*Hunter S. Thompson*
Comfortable	as a well-worn wellie.	*Anon.*
Comfortless	as frozen water to a starved snake.	*William Shakespeare*
Committee	a camel looks like a horse that was planned by a committee.	*Anon.*
Communism	might be likened to a race in which all competitors come in first, with no prizes.	*Lord Inchcape*
Communism	is like prohibition; it's a good idea, but it won't work.	*Will Rogers*
Comparing	comparing that with the . . . other . . . is like comparing Milton with Stilton.	*Dylan Thomas*

Compatible	as a mongoose and a cobra.	*Anon.*
Complexion	like an oxidised potato.	*Gerald Kersh*
Compliment	is something like a kiss through a veil.	*Victor Hugo*

Composure	effortless composure of a corpse in the morgue. *Raymond Chandler*
Conceited	like a cock who thought the sun had risen to hear him crow. *George Eliot*
Confident	as Crippen when he stood on the gallows. *Charlie Chester*
Confident	the confident spirit of an only child touching an indulgent father for chocolate cream. *P. G. Wodehouse*
Confined	like Jonah in a very narrow whale. *Jilly Cooper*
Confused	as a hedgehog in Reginald Bosanquet's dressing room. *Anon.*
Conservative	A conservative is like a player trying to steal second base while keeping his foot on first. *Laurence J. Peter*
Conservatives	They look rather like a collection of St Bernards that have lost their brandy. *Sir Harold Wilson*
Consistency	of a chameleon. *Anon.*
Conspicuous	like a moll at a christening. *Anon. (Australia)*
Conspicuous	as easy to spot as a kangaroo in a dinner jacket. *Raymond Chandler*
Conteh (John)	. . . a neck built like a stately home staircase. *Tom Davies*
Contented	as a cat eating hot mush on a frosty morning. *Nelson Algren*
Contrary	so contrary that if you threw him in the river he would float upstream. *Anon. (Ozark – USA)*
Controversial	as a cup final penalty. *Anon.*
Conversation	like hand-wrestling without the hands. *William McIlvanney*
Cool	as a knickerbocker glory. *Anon.*

Cool	as boarding house soup.	*Raymond Chandler*
Cool	as a cafeteria dinner.	*Raymond Chandler*

Cool	as a slice of chicken in aspic.	*Raymond Chandler*
Cool	as a trout.	*G. MacDonald Fraser*
Cool	as a moonbeam on a frozen brook.	*Oliver Wendell Holmes*
Cool	as some cucumbers.	*P. G. Wodehouse*
Corrupt	. . . utterly corrupt. Like rotten mackerel by moonlight he shines and stinks.	*John Randolph*
Cosset	like a prize leek.	*Anon.*
Cost-effective	as mink knickers.	*Katharine Whitehorn*
Cosy	as a sick kitten on a hot rock.	*Anon.*
Cough	like a cow who finds feathers mixed with hay.	*Honoré de Balzac*
Cough	like a sea lion peeved.	*Dylan Thomas*
Cough	. . . soft, low, gentle cough like a sheep with a blade of grass stuck in its throat.	*P. G. Wodehouse*

Crafty   as cheese.   *R. Creelman*

Cravat   . . . off-white . . . like whipped-up spud with a sort of
                      design made on it with a fork.   *Anthony Burgess*

Crazy   as two waltzing mice.   *Raymond Chandler*

Creased   as a sleeping boa-constrictor.   *William Matthews*

Creek   was like 12,845 telephone booths in a row with high
                      Victorian ceilings and all the doors taken off and all
                      the backs of the booths knocked out. *Richard Brautigan*

Cringe   like a toad under a harrow.   *Anon.*

Cringe   like a salted snail.   *P. G. Wodehouse*

Crisp   as a young lettuce.   *Anon.*

Critics   are like eunuchs in a harem: they know how it's
                      done, they've seen it done every day, but they're
                      unable to do it themselves.   *Brendan Behan*

Critics   are like brushers of noblemen's clothes.
                                                    Attrib. Sir Henry Wotton

Crooked   as a snake with the colic.   *Samuel Hopkin Adams*

Crooked   as a barrel of snakes.   *Anon. (Ozark – USA)*

Crooked   so crooked he sliced bread with a corkscrew.
                                                           P. G. Wodehouse

Crouch	like a frog on a telegraph pole.	*Anon.*
Cruel	The dirtiest Apache is a Christian gentleman compared to Moscon Ivery. He's as cruel as a snake and as deep as hell.	*John Buchan*
Cuckolded	antlered like a Tyrolean hunting lodge.	*Gerald Kersh*
Cumulus	streamed away under the fuselage like dissolving yoghurt.	*S. J. Perelman*
Cunning	as a dead pig.	*Anon.*
Curtains	net curtains that puckered in and out like the lips of a toothless old man sleeping.	*Raymond Chandler*
Cut	like a censor in a barber's shop.	*William Shakespeare*
Cute	as a bug's ear.	*Anon. (California)*
Cute	as a speckled pup under a red wagon.	*Anon. (California)*
Cute	as a couple of lost golf balls.	*Raymond Chandler*
Cute	as lace pants.	*Raymond Chandler*
Cute	as a washtub.	*Raymond Chandler*

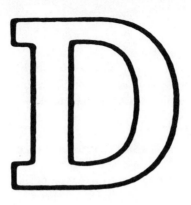

Dali (Salvador)	has a mind that works like a paranoic sponge.	*Anon.*
Damp	as a drowned hand.	*Gavin Lyall*
Dance	like an elephant with a hernia.	*Anon.*
Dance	like an Indian brave putting out a camp fire.	*Anon.*
Dance	like a hen on a hot griddle.	*Anon. (Scots)*
Dance	She swayed with him like blossom on a branch.	*George Mackay Brown*

Dance	I've seen the way he dances; it looks like something you do on Saint Walpurgis Night . . . being struck down dead would look like a day in the country compared to struggling out a dance with this boy. *Dorothy Parker*
Dance	like a dromedary with the staggers. *P. G. Wodehouse*
Dancing	She clapped me to her bosom like a belladonna plaster and pushed on the dance floor . . . it was like being lashed to an upholstered pneumatic drill. *Richard Gordon*
Dancing partner	like dragging the Statue of Liberty around the floor. *J. D. Salinger*
Dangerous	as an open man-hole. *Anon.*
Dangerous	as yellow kaffir dogs. *John Buchan*
Dangerous	on a par with taking a canoe trip to Dunkirk, during the evacuation. *Patrick Campbell*
Dangerous	full of dangerous energy, like a cobra listening to music. *Ross Macdonald*
Dangerous	like playing tennis with a hand-grenade. *William McIlvanney*
Dark	as the inside of a cow's stomach with her eye closed and her tail down. *Anon. (California)*
Dark	as a hog's ass. *Peter Benchley*
Dark	as the inside of a cabinet minister. *Joyce Cary*
Darker	than a yard down a bear's throat. *Damon Runyon*
Darkness	like the fruit of sloes, heavy and ripe to the touch. *Laurie Lee*
Dawn	breaks like a pomegranate . . . in a shining crack of red. *D. H. Lawrence*
Daybreak	arrived over the cemetery like a show of widespread indifference. *Leslie Thomas*

Days	slipped down like junket, leaving no taste on the tongue. *Betty MacDonald*
Days	There was nothing separate about her days; like drops upon a window-pane, they ran together and trickled away. *Dorothy Parker*
Dead	as a holiday resort in winter. *Anon.*
Dead	as last Christmas. *Raymond Chandler*
Dead	as a pickled walnut. *Raymond Chandler*
Dead	as a dog in a ditch. *Samuel Rowlands*
Dead beat	like something the bodysnatchers had thrown back in. *Gordon Williams*
Deaf	as an adder. *Anon.*
Deaf	as a haddock. *Anon.*
Death	is like the rumble of distant thunder at a picnic. *W. H. Auden*
Death	is on the air like the smell of ashes. *D. H. Lawrence*
Debonair	as a French count in a college play. *Raymond Chandler*
Deep	as a cup of tea. *Anon.*
Defenceless	as a tonsure. *Ross Macdonald*

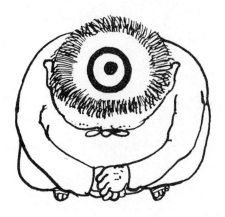

Defiance   . . . the conscious air of defiance that a waiter adopts in announcing that the cheapest priced claret on the wine-list is no more.   *Saki*

Deflated   looking like a bird of paradise that had been out all night in the rain.   *Oscar Wilde*

Delicate   as the play of moonbeams on a field of snow.
                                                                Robert B. Downs

Delicate   as a whisper.   *Cass McCallum*

Demeanour   . . . like Genghis Khan meditating a purge of his captains.   *Kingsley Amis*

Demeanour   his demeanour throughout was like that of a homicidal deaf mute.   *P. G. Wodehouse*

Demure   as an old whore at a baptism.   *Anon.*

Dentures   clicking like castanets, an old man chopped through a hot-dog at insect speed.   *Martin Amis*

Deport   She deported herself as aphrodisiacally as the law allowed.   *Peter de Vries*

Depressed   face like a fiddle.   *Anon.*

Design   not so much designed as congealed.   *Douglas Adams*

Desirable   as a blocked drain.   *Anon.*

Desk   that looked like Napoleon's tomb.   *Raymond Chandler*

Desk   about the size of a badminton court. *Raymond Chandler*

Despairing gesture like a vicar's daughter who has discovered Erastianism
                       in the village.   *P. G. Wodehouse*

Desperate remedy   like cutting your throat to cure a headache.   *Anon.*

Dialogue   as cryptic and formal as the ritual exchanges of
                       sentries.   *William McIlvanney*

Diamonds   enough ice . . . to cool the Mojave desert.
                                                                Raymond Chandler

Diet   . . . that produces the feeling of being locked in an
                       iron lung, with the machinery turned off.
                                                                  Patrick Campbell

Difficult   as grasping the small end of a hard-boiled egg. *Anon.*

Difficult   like trying to eat clear soup with chopsticks.   *Anon.*

Difficult   like trying to put a jersey on an octopus.
                                                                William McIlvanney

| Difficult | like trying to steal meat from a hammerhead shark. |
| | *Hunter S. Thompson* |

Difficult — like trying to steal meat from a hammerhead shark. *Hunter S. Thompson*

Diffident — as a collector for charity. *William McIlvanney*

Dignity — of an intoxicated dowager. *Raymond Chandler*

Dim — as a nun's nightlight. *Anon.*

Dim — as a Toc-H light. *Anon.*

Dinner conversation — was like Wimbledon, what with the swivelling heads. *Alida Baxter*

Dirty — looked like he was waylaid and raped by a gravedigger. *Richard Brautigan*

Disappear — like snow off a hot dyke. *Anon.*

Disappear — like icebergs in the Gulf Stream. *Richard Gordon*

Disappear — like eels into mud. *P. G. Wodehouse*

Disappointment — like going into Santa's grotto and finding a vending machine with a loudspeaker saying, 'Ho ho ho'. *John Timpson*

Disapproving — like a bishop finding a fly button in the collection. *David Niven*

Discreet — as a tombstone. *John Buchan*

Discreet — as a wink. *William McIlvanney*

Disdainful — as a dame who makes her dates by long distance. *Raymond Chandler*

Disdainful — . . . eyed the Scot as though he were one of the less publicised ingredients of haggis. *Richard Gordon*

Disgruntled — He made a noise like a pig swallowing half a cabbage. *P. G. Wodehouse*

Disgusted — with the expression of a man with a dead fish for a tie pin. *David Niven*

Disgusted   as if I had awoken in a bed full of vomit.
Jean-Paul Sartre

Disgusting   as hair in the butter.   *Anon.*

Dishevelled   as a bed in a cheap hotel.   *Nelson Algren*

Dismissive   as a teenage tomboy.   *Peter Peterson*

Disneyland   like being force-fed candyfloss.   *Ronnie Paris*

Distressed   as a cuckoo in the grip of a cat.   *Anon. (Sanskrit)*

Divine guidance If only God would give me some clear sign! Like
making a deposit in my name at a Swiss bank.
Woody Allen

Dizzy   as a dervish.   *Anon.*

Dog   like a hyperthyroid rat.   *Anon.*

Doleful   as a bullfrog crossed in love.   *Anon.*

Domestic   as a slipper.   *Dylan Thomas*

Door   opened hesitantly as if the place was coy about letting
you in.   *William McIlvanney*

Doorbell   . . .bing-bong; the kind of doorbell they have in
situation comedies about this kooky lady who lives
next door to her permanently-perplexed husband's ex-
wife.   *Keith Waterhouse*

Dowdy	. . . so dreadfully dowdy that she reminded one of a badly bound hymn-book.	*Oscar Wilde*
Drag	each minute dragged on him like an anchor dragging through gumbo mud.	*Ken Kesey*
Dragging	like a wounded snake.	*Alexander Pope*
Dread	He said it the way a sick man pronounces the name of his disease.	*Ross Macdonald*
Dreary	as a drowsy dromedary.	*John Heywood*
Dress	like a bell tent on legs.	*Anon.*
Dress	like a sow with sidepockets.	*Anon.*
Dressed up	like a pox-doctor's clerk.	*Anon.*
Dressed up	like a sore finger.	*Anon.*
Dressed up	like a turkey at Christmas.	*Anon.*
Dressed up	like Sugar Ray Robinson.	*Saul Bellow*
Dribble	This is a mess of a letter . . . it dribbles and mouths all over the place like Maurice Chevalier.	*Dylan Thomas*
Drink	the alcoholic equivalent of a mugging – expensive and bad for the head!	*Douglas Adams*
Drink	the effect of drinking a Pan Galactic Gargle Blaster is like having your brains smashed out by a slice of lemon wrapped round a large gold brick.	*Douglas Adams*
Drink	a pick-me-up strong enough to pop the pennies off the eyes of a dead Irishman.	*Anon.*
Drink	like a fish but not the same thing.	*Anon.*
Drink	like you've got a hollow leg.	*Anon.*
Drink	like there's no yesterday.	*Groucho Marx*

| Drinking | too much, not for pleasure, just sipping it systematically like low-proof hemlock. |
| | *William McIlvanney* |

| Driving (drunk) | as if he were tacking a sail boat.   *Raymond Chandler* |

| Drone | like a bankrupt dentist with toothache.   *Joyce Cary* |

| Droop | like a wax banana in a heat-wave.   *Denis Norden* |

| Drunk | as a skunk.   *Anon.* |

| Drunk | as a boiled owl.   *Anon. (Ozark – USA)* |

| Drunk | lit like a ferry boat.   *Raymond Chandler* |

| Drunk | as full as a pair of goats.   *Dashiell Hammett* |

Drunk	hooted as a foghorn	*Gavin Lyall*
Drunk	He pushed himself off the bar counter as if it was a jetty.	*William McIlvanney*
Drunk	as a deacon.	*Dylan Thomas*
Drunk	as a wheelbarrow.	*Samuel Wesley*
Dry	as Deuteronomy.	*Anon.*
Dry	as a prune.	*Anon.*
Dry	as a dead starfish.	*John Buchan*
Dry	as a bleached bone on a bone white beach.	*Anthony Burgess*
Dull	He's like a foggy day, dull and wet.	*Anon.*
Dull	as cold tea.	*Anon.*
Dull	as a widder-woman's ax.	*Anon. (Ozark – USA)*
Dull	as a mudflat.	*Maurice Hewlett*
Dull	as stale dogshit.	*Hunter S. Thompson*
Dumb	While he was not dumber than an ox, he was not any smarter.	*James Thurber*
Dynamic	as a ball bearing bouncing in a bathroom.	*Clive James*
Dynamic	as a pre-war kirby grip.	*Victoria Wood*

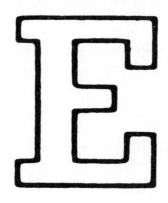

Eager   as a beaver on heat.   *Michael Bentine*

Earrings   jingling like tiny chandeliers.   *Anthony Burgess*

Ears   fuzz grew out of his ears, far enough to catch a moth.
Raymond Chandler

Ears   His ears make him look like a taxicab with both doors
open.   *Howard Hughes of Clark Gable*

Ears   like flying buttresses.   *Felicity Jones*

Ears   like the handles of a Greek amphora.
P. G. Wodehouse

Ease   all the ease of the Venus de Milo cracking a safe.
William McIlvanney

Easy   as opening an oyster with a bus ticket.   *Anon.*

Easy   as shinning up a thorn tree with an armload of eels.
Anon. (Ozark – USA)

Easy   It would be easier for Robert Morley to master hang-
gliding . . .   *John Naughton*

Eat   Redford fell upon his smoked salmon like a starved
dingo.   *Jilly Cooper*

Eat   like a cement mixer.   *B. J. Jones*

Eat   as if auditioning for Son of Billy Bunter.
William McIlvanney

Education	. . . like a Chinese meal: a succession of short courses and you never quite finish any of them. *Nicholas Coleridge*
Effective	as farting into the wind. *Anon.*
Effective	as peeing in the ocean. *Anon.*

Effective	as a sticking plaster for a severed jugular. *Anon.*
Effective	. . . as much effect as dropping a pebble off Beachy Head. *David Attenborough*
Elegant	as a refugee from Oliver Twist. *Anon.*
Elevator	rose as softly as the mercury in a thermometer. *Raymond Chandler*
Embarrassment	the blank embarrassment of a schoolboy suddenly called on to locate a minor prophet in the tangled hinterland of the Old Testament. *Saki*
Emotional	as a fish. *Anon.*
Emphasise	like a walk-on actress trying to make her name on the strength of a line. *William McIlvanney*
Emphatic	as a thunderclap. *Stella Gibbons*
Empty	as a dead man's eyes. *Anon. (Ozark – USA)*

Energy	They had squandered enough energy to build a couple of pyramids. *William McIlvanney*
English	The English treat their tailors as if they were clergymen . . . and their clergymen as if they were tailors. *Bob Scull*
English climate	on a fine day . . . is like looking up a chimney; on a foul day, like looking down one. *Anon.*
Enormous	'But she's so enormous,' he'd protest. 'In that lurex dress, it's like being out with a giant Brillo pad.' *Denis Norden*
Entertaining	as a bowl of cold porridge. *Anon.*
Enthusiasm	all the enthusiasm of a man about to handle a dead snake. *Groucho Marx*
Evil	as the eye of a hurricane. *Alan White*
Excited	like a Geiger counter in a Plutonium shop. *Kingsley Amis*
Exciting	as watching paint dry. *Anon.*
Exciting	as a wet November Sunday in Dunoon, with the only telephone kiosk broken. *Anon.*
Exciting	as the view inside a coffin. *Gavin Lyall*
Exciting	as two years of root canal treatments, on a dead fang. *John D. MacDonald*
Exciting	gets the adrenalin moving like a 440 volt blast in a copper bathtub. *Hunter S. Thompson*
Exclusive	as a mailbox. *Raymond Chandler*
Expectant	as joyfully expectant as Gordon of Khartoum. *Victoria Wood*
Expensive	as monogrammed caviare. *Anon.*

Experienced   seen more lovemaking than a policeman's torch.
                                                    Les Dawson

Expression   as much expression as a cut of round steak.
                                                    Raymond Chandler

Expressionless   as a cigar-store Indian.   *Raymond Chandler*

Extreme   like using a guillotine to cure dandruff.
                                                    Clare Boothe Luce

Eye   the kind that makes you reach up to see if your tie is
                      straight.   *P. G. Wodehouse*

Eyebrows   like the skins of some small mammal just not large
                      enough to be used as mats.   *Max Beerbohm*

Eyebrows   . . . raised up her brows like a chicken considering
                      something lying on the ground, not sure if it was just
                      a plain empty husk, or an interesting bit of nastiness.
                                                    Lewis Grassic Gibbon

Eyebrows   bristling like electrified hedgehogs.   *Richard Gordon*

Eyebrows   raised like rocketing pheasants.   *Richard Gordon*

Eyebrows   . . . rose slowly, reminding him of a pair of hairy
                      caterpillars crawling up a brick wall.   *Richard Gordon*

Eyebrows   working like a pair of battling stoats.   *Richard Gordon*

Eyelashes   looked like miniature iron railings.   *Raymond Chandler*

Eyelashes	long enough to catch flies.	*Clive James*
Eyelashes	that groped like furred antennae in the air.	
		Ross Macdonald
Eyelashes	as long as daisies.	*Edna O'Brien*
Eyelashes	sagging like display-window Christmas trees.	
		Tom Wolfe
Eyelids	When she raises her eyelids it's as if she were taking off all her clothes.	*Colette*
Eyes	glowed like two plums in a bowl of cream.	
		Nelson Algren

Eyes	blazing like chip pans.	*Anon.*
Eyes	like burnt holes in a blanket.	*Anon.*
Eyes	like peeled grapes.	*Anon.*
Eyes	like pissholes in the snow.	*Anon.*
Eyes	as brown as simulated teak filing cabinets.	*Sue Arnold*
Eyes	I have eyes like those of a dead pig.	*Marlon Brando*
Eyes	as dull as slate.	*Raymond Chandler*
Eyes	as shallow as a cafeteria tray or as deep as a hole to China – whichever you like.	*Raymond Chandler*
Eyes	like strange sins.	*Raymond Chandler*

Eyes   that had as much expression as the cap on a gas tank.
                                                        Raymond Chandler

Eyes   that looked as if they might warm up at the right time
                and in the right place.   *Raymond Chandler*

Eyes   with the sympathetic expression of wet stones.
                                                        Raymond Chandler

Eyes   enormous brown eyes, like hyperthyroid marbles.
                                                        Alistair Cooke

Eyes   gleaming and sparkling, like lizard's eyes in the
                crevices of old walls.   *A. Daudet*

Eyes   as pale as water in a china dish.   *G. MacDonald Fraser*

Eyes   Twin miracles of mascara, Barbara Cartland's eyes
                looked like two small crows that had crashed into a
                chalk cliff.   *Clive James*

Eyes   bright, brown – like a couple of cockroaches
                desperately swimming in two saucers of boiled
                rhubarb.   *Gerald Kersh*

Eyes   like he's been to the edge and looked over.   *Ken Kesey*

Eyes   bright as coins.   *Ross Macdonald*

Eyes   expanded like blue bubblegum bubbles.
                                                        Ross Macdonald

Eyes   like calculators.   *Ross Macdonald*

Eyes	like a poleaxed steer. *Ross Macdonald*
Eyes	like thin stab wounds filled with blood. *Ross Macdonald*
Eyes	bobbing like dead birds in a watertank. *Roger McGough*
Eyes	crawled like ants all over her. *William McIlvanney*
Eyes	flickered like those of a man watching trains go by. *William McIlvanney*
Eyes	His blue eyes turned on him like a blowtorch, lit but not yet shooting flame. *William McIlvanney*
Eyes	Her eyes made the blue of the Mediterranean look like pea soup. *W. Somerset Maugham*
Eyes	behind which emotions boiled like coffee under the glass knob of a percolator. *Peter de Vries*
Eyes	stood out like eggs in the wrong nest. *Peter de Vries*
Eyes	half veiled, like bluest waters seen through mists of rain. *Oscar Wilde*
Eyes	blazing like raccoons' at night by the garbage cans. *Tom Wolfe*
Eyes	like the bubbles in a carpenter's level. *Tom Wolfe*
Eye up	with all the modesty of peckish timber wolves. *Gordon Williams*

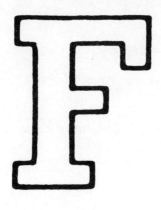

Face	like a bag of chisels.	*Anon.*
Face	like a bucket of mud.	*Anon.*
Face	like a coastguard station.	*Anon.*
Face	like a dish of tripe and onions.	*Anon.*
Face	like a milkman's round – long and dreary.	*Anon.*
Face	like a street before they lay the pavement.	*Anon.*
Face	like a tin of condemned veal.	*Anon.*
Face	like Louis Armstrong sucking a lemon with a steamroller going over his foot.	*Anon.*
Face	like the north end of a south-bound bus/cow.	*Anon.*

| Face | like the San Andreas Fault. | *Anon.* |
| Face | like yesterday's mince. | *Anon.* |

Face	like a half-chewed penny dainty. *Anon. (Glasgow)*
Face	a hard red face like a book of rules. *Anthony Carson*
Face	like what Cardinal Newman's would have been if he had gone into the army instead of the Church, grown an Old Bill moustache, lost most of his teeth, and only shaved on Saturdays, before preaching. *Joyce Cary*

Face	like a lost battle. *Raymond Chandler*
Face	like a face that had refused to gel and was about to run down on his clothes. *Irvin S. Cobb*
Face	like a three-day corpse. *G. MacDonald Fraser*
Face	like a squeezed orange. *Ben Jonson*
Face	as long as a late breakfast. *Anon.*
Face	I have a face like the behind of an elephant. *Charles Laughton*
Face	fell like a cookbook cake. *Joseph C. Lincoln*
Face	His face in repose was like an eroded landscape in a dry season. *Ross Macdonald*
Face	like a Barclaycard. *William McIlvanney*
Face	like a War Museum. *William McIlvanney*

Face	of a strong minded cow.	*George Orwell*

Face Her face, even with its powder, looked more than ever as if it should have been resting over the top rail of a paddock fence. *Dorothy Parker*

Face like a potato with mange. *Hunter S. Thompson*

Face like a monumental ruin of good looks. *Peter de Vries*

Face like a carving abandoned as altogether too unpromising for completion. *H. G. Wells*

Face His face had taken on the colour and expression of a devout tomato. *P. G. Wodehouse*

Face like a mixed grill. *Victoria Wood*

Fade like a morning dream. *Sir Compton Mackenzie*

Fade away like a pound of soap in a hard day's wash. *Anon.*

Faint as a fat lady at a fireman's ball. *Raymond Chandler*

Faint as a thumb print on a window pane. *Ross Macdonald*

Fair as picking pockets. *Anon.*

Faithful as the knee-joint to its socket. *Arthur Guiterman*

Falsity	in news is like rat droppings in clear soup. *Peking People's Daily*
Fame	like climbing a greasy pole for ten dollars and ruining trousers worth fifteen dollars. *Josh Billings*
Family	His family is like potatoes, all that is good of them are underground. *Anon.*
Fascinating	as a loose tooth. *Anon.*
Fast	as a jackrabbit in front of a prairie fire. *Anon.*
Fast	as a midge in a treacle pot. *Anon.*
Fast	as shit off a shiny shovel. *Anon.*
Fast	as a Yankee fakir selling patent pills. *G. MacDonald Fraser*
Faster	than a bishop from a brothel raid. *Anon.*
Fat	Flesh drips from me like hot fudge off a sundae . . . are there advantages or disadvantages to being built like a planet? *Woody Allen*

Fat	Just take Winnie; Like a barracks in a pinny, Gave up food for Lent, Weight loss was fantastic, But her skin was not elastic, Like an inefficient camper in a creased pink tent. *Victoria Wood*

Fear	shook through me. It was just like a crystal chandelier made out of adrenalin swaying wildly in an earthquake.	*Richard Brautigan*
Fear	hissed like escaping gas in his voice.	*Ross Macdonald*
Features	resembled a fossilised washrag.	*Alan Brien of Steve McQueen*
Fickle	as a weather vane.	*Anon.*
Fight	like a threshing machine.	*Anon.*
Fight	like a wild dog drunk on slaughterhouse blood.	*Woody Guthrie*
Fight	like a welterweight cinnamon bear.	*O. Henry*
Figure	as full of curves as a scenic railway.	*P. G. Wodehouse*
Fine	as a cow turd stuck with primroses.	*Anon.*
Fingernails	like the Bride of Dracula.	*Carol Bunyan*
Fingernails	like pearlised pink tusks.	*Gordon Burn*
Fingernails	like a split bud of a black fuchsia just about to open.	*Ole-Luk-Oie*
Fingernails	of so thick and glistening a red that it seemed as she but recently had completed tearing an ox apart with her naked hands.	*Dorothy Parker*
Fingers	pale and speckled like breakfast sausages.	*Ross Macdonald*
Fireproof	as a delicatessen bag.	*Raymond Chandler*
Fishy	as Dick's hatband.	*Anon.*
Fit	as a butcher's dog.	*Anon.*
Fit	as a fritter for a friar's mouth.	*Anon.*
Flash	as a rat with a gold tooth.	*Anon. (Australia)*

Flat	as a filleted flounder.	*Anon.*
Flat	and stale as a football interview.	*Raymond Chandler*
Flat	as a crêpe suzette.	*P. G. Wodehouse*
Flat out	like a lizard drinking.	*Anon. (Australia)*
Flatten	I flattened him like a welcome mat.	*Damon Runyon*
Flee	like a rat down a pipe.	*Anon.*
Fleshless	as a mummy.	*Evelyn Waugh*
Float	like a butterfly, sting like a bee.	*'Bundini' Brown*
Flustered	as a side of beef.	*Raymond Chandler*
Flutter	like a butterfly caught in a shutter.	*Anon.*
Fly	Put cream and sugar on a fly, and it tastes very much like a black raspberry.	*Edgar W. Howe*
Folkestone	lay along the cliffs like a Victorian matron, dabbling her toes in the sea.	*Michael Bentine*
Follow	like buzzards after a gut-wagon.	*Anon. (Ozark – USA)*
Follow	like an old weasel tracing a rat.	*J. M. Synge*
Food	tasted like a discarded mail bag.	*Raymond Chandler*

Football tackle   like a road accident.   *David Lacey*

Football team   like an old bra – no cups and hardly any support.
                                                                      Anon.

Footsteps   echoed away like a woodpecker falling asleep.
                                                                      Boris Vian

Forearm   smooth and tepid as a new laid brown egg.
                                                                      Anthony Burgess

Forehead   . . . a blond pompadour whose wavelets lapped a
                         forehead narrower than Ronald Reagan's.
                                                                      S. J. Perelman

Forlorn   like a dying duck in a thunderstorm.   *Anon.*

Forlorn   as a lost goose.   *Anon. (Ozark – USA)*

Formalised   as a page of *Marius the Epicurean*.   *Raymond Chandler*

Fornication   galloping away like an archdeacon on holiday.
                                                                      G. MacDonald Fraser

Fornication   thrashing away like a stoat in a sack.
                                                                      G. MacDonald Fraser

Frail   like a couple of eye sockets mounted on a piece of
                         modern solder sculpture.   *Tom Wolfe*

Frantically   like it was going out of fashion.   *Anon.*

Freckles	like a mine-field on a war map.	*Raymond Chandler*
Free	as a bird sprung from a cage.	*Anon.*
Free verse	Writing free verse is like playing tennis with the net down.	*Robert Frost*
Fresh	as lollipops.	*Tom Davies*
Fresh	as fruit salad.	*Cordelia Oliver*
Fresh	as a dewy violet.	*P. G. Wodehouse*
Fretful	as a bear with a sore ear.	*Anon.*
Friendless	as an alarm clock.	*Anon.*
Friendly	as a shark with toothache.	*Anon.*
Friendly	as castrating knives.	*Alida Baxter*
Friendly	as a chain gang boss.	*Woody Guthrie*
Friendly	as a Saint Bernard puppy.	*Dashiell Hammett*
Friendly	as rabid wolves.	*Ken Kesey*
Friendship	The feeling of friendship is like that of being comfortably filled with roast beef.	*Dr Johnson*

Frightened	. . . had reduced me to the consistency of calf's-foot jelly.	*S. J. Perelman*
Frightening	as Donald Duck.	*Kingsley Amis*
Frost	on the grass like condensed moonlight.	*Joyce Cary*
Frown	a persistent troubled frown which gave him the expression of someone who is trying to repair a watch with his gloves on.	*James Thurber*
Frugally	as a European bus conductor making change.	*Joseph Heller*
Full	as a lovebird's egg.	*Dylan Thomas*
Fuller	than a pomegranate is of pips.	*Douglas Adams*
Fun	more fun than a barrel of monkeys.	*Anon.*
Fun	more fun than a frog in a plate of warm water.	*Anon.*
Fun	no more fun than a sinus wash.	*Clive James*
Fun	As a source of entertainment, conviviality and good fun, she ranks somewhere between a sprig of parsley and a single ice skate . . . she is about as hot company as a night-nurse.	*Dorothy Parker*
Fun	as much fun as phlegm.	*Victoria Wood*
Fun-loving	even at my most unbuttoned, I am to the Fun People what Marcel Marceau is to radio.	*Denis Norden*
Funny	as a crutch.	*Anon.*
Funny	as an armpit with a boil.	*Charlie Chester*
Funny	as gangrene.	*William McIlvanney*
Furtive	as a set of false whiskers.	*Dashiell Hammett*
Fury	flared up in his mind like forgotten toast under a grill.	*Kingsley Amis*
Fuss	more fuss than a skunk in a henhouse.	*Anon.*

Fussed over   like a black guest at an anti-apartheid garden party.

Graham Greene

Futile   like rabbit-hunting with a dead ferret.   *Anon.*

Futile   as a clock in an empty house.   *James Thurber*

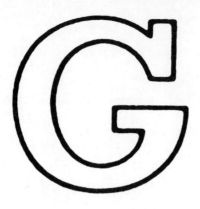

Gall	of a shoplifter returning an item for a refund.	*W. I. E. Gates*
Gangling	in repose I looked like a pair of discarded braces.	*Denis Norden*
Gasp	like a man trying to gargle whilst fighting off a pack of wolves.	*Douglas Adams*
Gasping	like a grouse on the Glorious Twelfth.	*Anon.*
Gasping	like a cod in a goldfish bowl.	*Felicity Jones*
Gasping	like a frog in a drought.	*C. Kingsley*
Gaudy	as a chiropractor's chart.	*Raymond Chandler*
Gay	as a goose in a gutter.	*Anon.*
Gay	as superannuated streetwalkers.	*Raymond Chandler*
Gaze	like an ostrich goggling at a brass door-knob.	*P. G. Wodehouse*
Gentle	as a Brillo pad.	*Anon.*
Gentle	as fingers touching a wound.	*William McIlvanney*
Gently	as an old maid stroking a cat.	*Raymond Chandler*
Gesticulate	like a conductor leading an orchestra in a prolonged discord.	*Peter de Vries*
Get on	like ham and eggs.	*Anon.*
Get on	like port and nuts.	*Anon.*

Get on	like a piece of damp blotting paper on fire. *Jilly Cooper*
Glance	A ninety-degree glance around the bar, as casual as a turtle with inflamed neck glands. *Keith Waterhouse*
Gleam	like minnows in a rain barrel. *Anon. (USA)*
Gleam	like a bride in a mirror. *R. D. Blackmore*
Glib	He could shed words glibly as a frog spawns. *Gerald Kersh*
Gloomy	. . . resemblance to a frog which had been looking on the dark side since it was a slip of a tadpole. *P. G. Wodehouse*
Glum	. . . a bloke who habitually looks like a pterodactyl that has suffered. *P. G. Wodehouse*
Glutinous	so glutinous it could induce lockjaw in a mule. *Clive James*

Gnaw	like a burning worm.	*John Bunyan*

Go Be cool and quick to go
As a drop of April snow. *Dorothy Parker*

Goggling like a bulldog confronted with a pound of steak.
P. G. Wodehouse

Golf is like a love affair: if you don't take it seriously it's no
fun; if you do take it seriously, it breaks your heart.
Arnold Daly

Golf course as unplayable as Mount Everest. *Patrick Campbell*

Golf swing My back swing off the first tee had put him in mind
of an elderly woman of dubious morals trying to
struggle out of a dress too tight around the shoulders.
Patrick Campbell

Gown like an Arthur Rackham soul bird. *Tom Wolfe*

Grab like a seagull at a crust. *George Mackay Brown*

Graceful as a gouty hippo. *Anon.*

Graceful as a Chopin ending. *Raymond Chandler*

Grant (Cary) this great sun-tan that looks like it was done on a
rotisserie. *Tom Wolfe*

Greasy hair like a spaniel that drowned in a chip pan.
Victoria Wood

Greedy	as ten cocks scraping in a dunghill for a barley pickle.
	Anon. (Scots)
Greedy	as a weasel in a hen-house. *Anon.*
Green	as gooseshit. *Anon. (Ozark – USA)*
Green	as a starboard light. *Joyce Cary*

Greer (Germaine)	Despite a lifetime of service to the cause of sexual liberation, I have never caught a venereal disease, which makes me feel rather like an arctic explorer who has never had frostbite. *Germaine Greer*
Grey	Misty grey like cows' breath on a frosty morning.
	Irvin S. Cobb
Grin	like a basket of chips. *Anon.*
Grin	like a Cheshire cat chewing gravel. *Anon.*
Grin	as lewd as a satyr's. *Dashiell Hammett*
Grin	so wide he looked like a Hammond organ.
	David Niven
Grinning	like a big baboon picking lice. *Ed McBain*
Groan	like a convalescent rooster learning to crow again after a long illness. *Raymond Chandler*
Groan	He groaned softly and winced, like Prometheus watching his vulture dropping in for lunch.
	P. G. Wodehouse

Grousing	like a labour battalion.
	John Buchan
Guest	A guest, like a fish, has an unpleasant odour after three days.
	Guido Cavalenti
Guinness	The top of the drink was like the full moon. The rest of it was as black and soft and mild as a West Cork night after the moon has set, early in the springtime of the year.
	Patrick Skene Catling
Gums	bare gums like polished coral.
	Anthony Burgess
Gun	bulging like a benign tumour in my armpit.
	Ross Macdonald
Gunfire	as if nocturnal women were beating great carpets.
	Virginia Woolf
Gusto	Buller [the boxer dog] was licking his private parts with the gusto of an alderman drinking soup.
	Graham Greene

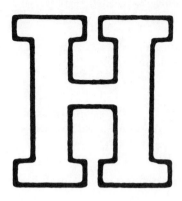

H

Hair　　　　My hair hung on my head as if it were a cut-price toupee. *Martin Amis*

Hair　　　　like an owl in an ivy-bush. *Anon.*

Hair　　　　like Our Lord's donkey. *Anon. (Liverpool)*

Hair　　　　like crisps. *Alida Baxter*

Hair　　　　like Persian lambs' fur. *Saul Bellow*

Hair　　　　as red as chili powder. *Saul Bellow*

Hair　　　　a brush of erect grey hair, like iron filings tempted by a magnet. *Ross Macdonald*

Hair　　　　sticking out like a sweep's brush dipped in sump oil. *Frank Muir*

Hair　　　　Her hair had the various hues of neglected brass. *Dorothy Parker*

Hair   long honeyed strands like the furrows that a happy
                            farmer ploughs through apricot jam with his fork.
                                                                                Boris Vian

Hair   A black jungle of it, coming to a point at the front
                            between deepening bald wedges, looking like half a
                            slice of burnt toast.   *Peter de Vries*

Hair   sufficiently pomaded to stain his hat band like a
                            doughnut bag.   *Peter de Vries*

Haircut   looked like an aircraft carrier for flies.   *Clive James*

Hairs   as thick as tooth-picks.   *Kingsley Amis*

Hairstyle   . . . squashed spider plastered on his brow.
                                                                            Russell Davies

Hand (of cards)   a hand like a foot.   *Anon.*

Hand   as clammy as a wet fish.   *Anon.*

Hand   as stiff and brittle as an antlered ring stand.
                                                                            Anthony Burgess

Hand   like a fat maggot.   *Jean-Paul Sartre*

Hand out drinks   like his own blood.   *Sir Compton Mackenzie*

Hands   as pudgy as baseball mitts.   *Alistair Cooke*

Hands   clasped like children lost in a wood.   *Sean O'Faolain*

Hands	twitched and plucked at each other like nervous scorpions.	*Ross Macdonald*
Handshake	The feel of it was of a bundle of dry sticks in a bag.	*G. MacDonald Fraser*
Handshake	like milking a cow.	*Gavin Lyall*
Handshake	like a canvas glove full of hot sand.	*John D. MacDonald*
Handshake	The kind of handshake that ought never to be used except as a tourniquet.	*Denis Norden*
Handwriting	like the lesser rivers on maps.	*Dorothy Parker*
Handwriting	Your handwriting makes even a simple address look like a nice Sanskrit poem.	*Dylan Thomas*
Handy	as a pig with a musket.	*Anon.*
Handy	as a pocket in a shirt.	*Anon.*
Hangover	mouth like a Russian/Turkish/Sumo wrestler's jockstrap.	*Anon.*
Hangover	a head like an open wound.	*Raymond Chandler*
Hangover	I felt like an amputated leg.	*Raymond Chandler*
Hangover	like twelve Swedes.	*Raymond Chandler*

| Hangover | My brain felt like a bucket of wet sand. |
| | *Raymond Chandler* |

Hangover | that ought to be in the Smithsonian Institution under glass. *Dorothy Parker*

Hangover | a head like a windmill. *Dylan Thomas*

Hangover | a head like a box of hungry woodpeckers. *Gordon Williams*

Happiness | is an extremely simple affair – like pulling a plug when the birds are singing. *Anthony Carson*

Happiness | is like coke – something you get as a by-product in the process of making something else. *Aldous Huxley*

Happy | like a man interrupted at his investiture with the Order of Merit to be told that a six-figure cheque from a football pool awaits him in the lobby. *Kingsley Amis*

Happy | as a bastard on father's day. *Anon.*

Happy | as a clam at high tide. *Anon.*

Happy | as a pig in a pork pie factory. *Anon.*

Happy | as a pig in shit. *Anon.*

Happy | as baby beavers in a toothpick factory. *Anon.*

Happy | as a possum up a gum tree. *Anon. (Australia)*

Happy | as a dead pig in the sunshine. *Anon. (Ozark – USA)*

Happy | as a heifer in a corncrib. *Anon. (Ozark – USA)*

Happy | as a monkey in a monkey tree. *Randy Newman*

Happy | as nine dollars worth of lettuce. *Damon Runyon*

Happy | as the sunshine of St Martin's Day. *J. M. Synge*

Happy | as a louse on a dirty head. *Paul Theroux*

Happy	I believe with all my heart that we'll live together one day as happily as two lobsters in a saucepan, two bugs on a muscle, one smile, though never to vanish, on the Cheshire face. *Dylan Thomas*
Hard	as a cold slab. *C. E. Beilby*
Hard boiled	He [Dashiell Hammett] is so hard boiled you could roll him on the White House lawn. *Dorothy Parker*
Harmless	as a sleeping cat. *Anon.*

Harmless	as a powder magazine built over a match factory. *James Dunne*
Harmless	as boiled milk. *Anon.*
Hat	looking like a beehive splattered with custard. *Patrick Campbell*
Hat	that had been taken from its mother too young. *Raymond Chandler*
Hat	He threw off his hat like a catcher going after a high one. *Peter de Vries*
Hate	Hating people is like burning down your own house to get rid of a rat. *Harry Emerson Fosdick*
Hatred	rose in him like black vomit. *Anthony Burgess*
Head	like a rosary bead. *Anon. (Liverpool)*
Head	like a Spanish onion. *P. G. Wodehouse*

Headache	a yard wide.	*Raymond Chandler*
Headlights (in fog)	Headlights swarm in pairs like deep sea fish.	*Ross Macdonald*
Healthy	as an alligator.	*Anon. (Ozark – USA)*
Heart	like a lonesome gravestone.	*Nelson Algren*
Heart	as big as one of Mae West's hips.	*Raymond Chandler*
Heart	Her heart, soft and sweet as a perfectly made crème renversée, quivered in her breast.	*Dorothy Parker*
Heart	I wore my heart like a wet red stain on the breast of a velvet gown.	*Dorothy Parker*
Hesitate	like one o'clock half struck.	*Anon.*
Hi-fi	the sort of vastly elaborate hi-fi system you need a licence to drive.	*Jilly Cooper*
High	like a ping pong ball on a water jet.	*David Niven*
High	jacked up like the great hummingbird.	*Hunter S. Thompson*
Higher	than a cat's back.	*Damon Runyon*
Hilarity	like a scream from a crevasse.	*Graham Greene*

Himmler	Close-ups of Himmler's crew-cut head looking as if a bag of suet had been crammed into a pencil sharpener. *Clive James*
Hips	spread like a tub of dough in a bakehouse. *Gerald Kersh*
Hobnob	like a couple of sailors on shore leave. *P. G. Wodehouse*
Hold	as if it was a two-week-dead lark. *Douglas Adams*
Hole	as yawning as the centre of a Claes Oldenberg doughnut. *Philip French*
Hopeful	like a struggling spiritualist slipping her card into a passing coffin. *Derek Marlowe*
Hopeless	like trying to convince an eight year old that sexual intercourse is more fun than a chocolate ice cream cone. *Howard Gossage*
Hopeless	like four-nothing with two minutes to go. *William McIlvanney*
Horny	as a hoot owl. *Anon.*
Horny	as the town bull. *G. MacDonald Fraser*
Horror story	The tone of it will be so quiet that the horror should rise up like a clot of blood in the throat. *Dylan Thomas*
Hot	as a fire in a pepper mill. *Anon. (Ozark – USA)*
Hot	as a hen laying a goose egg. *Anon. (Ozark – USA)*
Hot	as a flush. *R. Beak*
Hot	hotter than a ninth inning finish. *Damon Runyon*
Hot	so hot you could fry an egg on any part of him. *Damon Runyon*
Hot	My brains are hanging out like the intestines of a rabbit. . . . My tongue . . . is as hot as a camel-saddle mounted by baked Bedouins. My eyes like over-ripe tomatoes strain at the sweating glass of a Saharan hothouse. *Dylan Thomas*

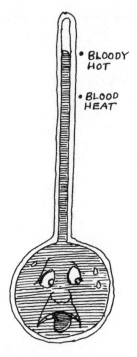

BLOODY
HOT

BLOOD
HEAT

Hot and bothered	like lobsters on the way to the steam bath. *Bob Hope*
House of Lords	– a perfect eventide home. *Lady Stocks*
Hover	like a bird near a slaughterhouse. *Anon. (Sanskrit)*
Hug	squeezed a groan out of me like a note out of an accordion. *Peter de Vries*
Human history	the story of an ape playing with a box of matches on a petrol dump. *David Ormsby Gore*
Humming	sounded like a cow being sick. *Raymond Chandler*
Humour	went down like a brick parachute. *Anon.*
Hungry	as a June crow. *Anon.*
Hungry	hollow as the Grand Canyon. *P. G. Wodehouse*
Hungry	like a python when the zoo officials have started to bang the luncheon gong. *P. G. Wodehouse*

Hurt   feel like a wellington filled with blood.   *Adrian Henri*

Hygiene   like a spittoon in a Turkish brothel.   *Anon.*

Hysterical   as a tree full of chickens.   *Irvin S. Cobb*

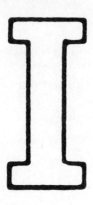

Ideals	living up to your ideals is like doing everyday work with your Sunday clothes on. *Ed Howe*
Ideas	buzzed like a swarm without a hive. *Peter de Vries*
Ignored	like a bastard cousin at a family reunion. *Anon.*
Impertinent	more neck than a giraffe. *Anon.*
Impertinent	like a sparrow trying to intimidate a buzz-saw. *William McIlvanney*
Implications	jostled impossibly in his mind like a football crowd all trying to get through the boys' gate at one time. *William McIlvanney*
In and out	like a French farce. *Anon.*
Inappropriate	like widow's weeds on a virgin. *William McIlvanney*
Incommoding	as Olympic high-jumping in plus fours. *Patrick Campbell*
Incongruous	as a blacksmith with a white silk apron. *Anon.*
Inconspicuous	as a privy on the front lawn. *Raymond Chandler*
Inconspicuous	as a tarantula on a slice of angel food. *Raymond Chandler*
Inconspicuous	as the Invisible Man. *Clive James*

Indignant	as though he had been drowning and a life-guard had informed him he would save him tomorrow. *Clarence Day*
Indulge	like a dog rolling in muck. *Alida Baxter*
Ineffectual	like being savaged by a dead sheep. *Denis Healey (on an attack by Sir Geoffrey Howe)*
Inflexible	as an epitaph. *William McIlvanney*
Informal	as a Polish wedding. *Anon.*
Innocent	We looked at each other with the clear innocent eyes of a couple of used-car salesmen. *Raymond Chandler*
Innocent	as Queen Victoria when young. *Clive James*
Innocent	She was as ignorant of the give-and-take of the kiss as a Polynesian with a hibiscus in her ear. *Gerald Kersh*
Innocent	like a virgin at a Freshman tea. *Ed McBain*

Innocent	like Snow White.	*William McIlvanney*
Innocuous	as a dose of the flu.	*Archie Macpherson*
Inseparable	as a football fan and a hot meat pie.	*Anon.*

Intelligence tests
. . .remind me of the way they used to weigh hogs in Texas. They would get a long plank, put it over a crossbar, and somehow tie the hog on one end of the plank. They'd search all around till they found a stone that would balance the weight of the hog and they'd put that on the other end of the plank. Then they'd guess the weight of the stone. *John Dewey*

Intelligent	as a lobotomised prawn.	*Anon.*
Intelligent	as bright as a blackout.	*Anon.*
Interest	of a dead goldfish.	*Raymond Chandler*
Interesting	as trying to date a nun.	*Anon.*
Interesting	as watching a plank warp.	*Anon.*

Interesting
like being the film star's fifth husband; you know what to do, the problem's making it interesting.
Anon.

Intermittently	like the click of a blind man's cane.	*Irvin S. Cobb*

Interpreter
To work through an interpreter is like hacking one's way through a forest with a feather. *James Evans*

Intimacies
sprang up in the crevices of darkness like tropical flowers. *William McIlvanney*

Intimate	as the rustle of sheets.	*Dorothy Parker*
Inviting	as a postcard.	*Richard Brautigan*
Invulnerable	as my great-great-grandfather.	*Raymond Chandler*

Irrational
like turning down Hawaii for a weekend in Arran.
William McIlvanney

Irrelevant

The Marxist analysis has got nothing to do with what happened in Stalin's Russia; it's like blaming Jesus Christ for the Inquisition in Spain.
Tony Benn

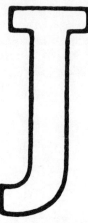

Jaw   like a park bench.   *Raymond Chandler*

Jealous   as a couple of hairdressers.   *R. C. Trench*

Jealous   as the Mona Lisa's sister.   *Ronnie Paris*

Jellyfish   like a striped red blister.   *Jilly Cooper*

Jerky   as a clockwork snake.   *H. G. Wells*

Jewelled   So covered with diamonds and jewels that he looks as if he has been caught in a rain of them and come in dripping.   *Caryl Brahms and S. J. Simon*

Jewelled   . . . a large, pleasant chandelier of a woman, covered with costume jewellery. It kept falling off her like decorations from a Christmas tree.   *Peter de Vries*

Joie de vivre   all the joie de vivre of a half-eaten meat-and-potato pie.   *Victoria Wood*

Joint   She handed him a joint so ill-made that it resembled a baby's winkle.   *Martin Amis*

Joseph (Sir Keith)   . . . like the conjurer who took a beautiful watch from a member of the audience, hid it in a handkerchief, smashed it to smithereens with a mallet and then told the crowd: 'I am sorry, I have forgotten the rest of the trick.'   *Michael Foot*

Journalism   The art of newspaper paragraphing is to stroke a platitude until it purrs like an epigram.   *Don Marquis*

Joyous   like a choir-boy when the paid tenor comes in wrong.   *Joyce Cary*

Jump	like the Statue of Liberty stung by a mosquito.
	P. G. Wodehouse
Jumping	like a toad in a thunderstorm. *Anon.*
Jumping	like a Mexican bean in a bassoon. *Patrick Campbell*
Jump on	like a duck on a June bug. *Anon.*
Jumpy	as a pea on a drum. *Anon.*
Jumpy	like you had a cricket in each pocket. *Norman Mailer*
Jungle	Moving in this jungle was like searching in a big attic closet on a summer morning, old moist bathrobes drawing across one's face and rusty old clothes hangers snagging in one's hair, corrugated cardboard beneath one's feet. *John Sack*

JUST LIKE THAT!

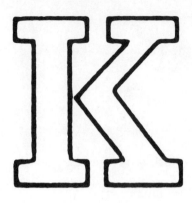

Kind	as a turtle.	*Anon.*
Kinky	as a very old dancing pump.	*Clive James*
Kiss	like tyre explosions.	*Anon.*
Kiss	as though he was trying to clear the drains.	*Alida Baxter*
Kiss	like eating purple plums.	*George Mackay Brown*
Kiss	lipping her absently like a goldfish.	*William McIlvanney*
Kiss	that reduced my bones to rubber and my brain to gruel.	*Peter de Vries*
Knee	like the corner of a foundation stone.	*Raymond Chandler*
Knees	His bony knees vibrated like tuning forks.	*Ross Macdonald*

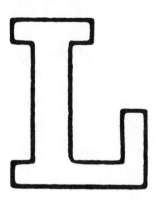

Large   as life and in fact twenty pounds larger.

Damon Runyon

Laugh   like rain water pouring over daffodils made from silver.   *Richard Brautigan*

Laugh   like a blackbird in a bush.   *D. H. Lawrence*

Laugh   like a bowlful of jelly.   *Clement C. Moore*

Laugh   . . . a laugh so hearty it knocks the cream off an order of strawberry shortcake on a table fifty yards away

Damon Runyon

Laugh   like a hyena with a bone stuck in its throat.

P. G. Wodehouse

Laugh   like a train going into a tunnel.   *P. G. Wodehouse*

Laugh   like a troop of cavalry galloping over a tin bridge.

P. G. Wodehouse

Laugh	like waves breaking on a stern and rock-bound coast. *P. G. Wodehouse*
Laughing	like seven hyenas turned inside out and covered with chicken feathers. *Richard Brautigan*
Laughing	like a hen having hiccups. *Raymond Chandler*
Laughter	rang like cracked bells. *Ross Macdonald*
Lawn	flowed like a cool green tide. *Raymond Chandler*
Laws	. . . like cobwebs; where the small flies are caught and the great break through. *Francis Bacon*
Lawyer	Being a lawyer in Beverley Hills must be the closest thing to being a landed squire in eighteenth century England. *Erica Jong*
Lawyer	Being a lawyer is like being a bottle of ketchup in a restaurant that specialises in bad steaks. It covers a multitude of sins. *Jerome Weidman*
Lawyers	Woodpeckers and lawyers have long bills. *C. K. Allen*
Lawyers	A countryman between two lawyers is like a fish between two cats. *Benjamin Franklin*
Lay abed	Spread like soft butter on warm toast, his body trickling gratefully into the folds of blanket and counterpane. *Martin Amis*
Lazy	as a day in June. *Anon.*
Lazy	as a toad at the bottom of a well. *Anon.*
Lazy	like Ludham's dog that leaned his head against the wall to bark. *Thomas Fuller*
Lean	as a streak. *Anon.*
Leap	like a salmon in spawning season. *P. G. Wodehouse*
Leave	They shrank from him like wraiths of mist from the cliffs. *George Mackay Brown*

Leave   He slipped quietly away, like a host who feels that a
                   house party will get on much better without him.
                                                      Graham Greene

Legitimate   as lechery.   *Gavin Lyall*

Legs   Thick ankles and thin thighs, like she had her legs on
                   upside down.   *Anon.*

Legs   Beef to the heels, like a Mullinger heifer.   *Anon. (Irish)*

Legs   When she got up, her legs twinkled through the
                   dining room like swords.   *Anthony Carson*

Legs   like a Bavarian bullock.   *David Niven*

Levin (Bernard) . . . squeaking away in the undergrowth like a
                   demented vole.   *Denis Healey*

Lie   like a hairy egg.   *Anon.*

Lie   like a man with a secondhand car.   *Anon.*

Lie   like a road casualty.   *Beryl Bainbridge*

Life   will crush you like an empty beer can.   *Saul Bellow*

Life   is rather like a tin of sardines – we're all of us looking
                   for the key.   *Alan Bennett*

Life   is like an ashtray, full of little dowts.   *Billy Connolly*

Life   is like eating artichokes – you've got to go through so
                   much to get so little.   *T. A. Dorgan*

Life	as much life in him as the House of Lords on Derby Day. *Dick Emery*
Life	is like a football game with everyone offside and the referee gotten rid of – everyone claiming the referee would have been on his side. *F. Scott Fitzgerald*
Life	is like a reversible coat – seamy on both sides. *O. Henry*
Lift	as hard to lift as a dead elephant. *Raymond Chandler*
Lightning	like some whimsical and very wicked marmalade. *Peter de Vries*
Lights	shone like wit in a dowager. *Ross Macdonald*
Like	like the devil likes holy water. *Anon.*
Likely	. . . no more . . . than to find Gibbon's *History of Christianity* in my navel. *Dylan Thomas*
Limousine	making a noise like dead leaves falling. *Raymond Chandler*
Limp	as a scrubwoman's back hair. *Raymond Chandler*
Limp	as a wet noodle. *Robert Coover*
Lips	as shiny as Tiptree's strawberry jam. *Cecil Beaton (of Tallulah Bankhead)*
Lips	of slack red meat. *Anthony Burgess*
Lips	Her lips always looked as if someone had just pulled a trombone from her. *Denis Norden*
Lips	hang off his face like giblets. *Tom Wolfe (of Mick Jagger)*
Liqueur	tasted like nose-drops. *Peter de Vries*
Listen	They licked up his sermon like calves at a cog. *Lewis Grassic Gibbon*
Literary appreciation	She doesn't understand my writing and said last night that my 'Critique of Metaphysical Reality' reminded her of *Airport*. *Woody Allen*

Lively	as a wet night at Stonehenge	*Richard Gordon*
Loathsome looking	a cross between an orgy scene in the movies and some low form of pond life.	*P. G. Wodehouse*
Lobby	not quite as big as the Yankee Stadium.	*Raymond Chandler*
Lonely	as a milestone.	*Anon.*
Lonely	as lighthouses.	*Raymond Chandler*
Lonely	as flagpole sitting.	*Ben Hecht*
Lonely	Hard and lonely as an old pit dog.	*Ken Kesey*
Lonely	as a crow on the sands.	*William Wordsworth*

Long	as King Kong's prick.	*R. J. Serling*
Long	as a well-rope.	*Anon. (Ozark – USA)*
Long	as a Thanksgiving sermon.	*Anon. (USA)*
Longwinded	as a tornado.	*Anon.*
Look	at him as if he were something she had trodden in.	*Anon.*
Look	at him as if he were something the cat had brought in/ thrown up.	*Anon.*

Look	A look that felt like a dentist's drill. *Raymond Chandler*
Look	She looks at other women as though she would inhale them. *Ronald Firbank*
Look	A look like a noose. *Victor Hugo*
Look	A look you could pour on a waffle. *Ring Lardner*
Look	like a professor of English Literature who has not approved of the writings of anybody since Sir Thomas Browne. *James Thurber*
Loose	as a goose. *Anon. (Ozark – USA)*
Loose	as concrete. *Damon Runyon*
Lost	as a lump of butter in a greyhound's throat. *Anon.*
Lost	like beads off a string. *Anon.*
Lost	like Alexander, with no more worlds to conquer. *D. H. Lawrence*
Loud	as a gnat snapping its fingers. *Simon Hoggart*
Love	had germinated like a seed in the dark. *John Buchan*
Love affair	that made Vesuvius look like a damp sparkler. *Alida Baxter*
Lovemaking	They made love as though they were an endangered species. *Peter de Vries*

Low	as a centipede with fallen arches. *Anon.*
Low	as a snake's belly. *Anon.*
Low	so low he could have walked under a snake with a top hat on. *Anon.*
Low	as a badger's belly. *Raymond Chandler*
Lumberjack	like a Kodiak bear someone had succeeded in partially shaving and getting into a dirty sweat shirt. *Ken Kesey*
Lungs (smokers')	like whale blubber full of big black holes. *Stanley Eveling*

McEnroe (John)	hair like badly bound broccoli.	*Clive James*
Mad	as a wet hen.	*Anon.*
Mad	as a cut snake.	*Anon. (Australia)*
Maidenhead	Frankly, the rupturing of my maidenhead had been just about as meaningful as the breaking of a paper saniband on a motel toilet.	*Lisa Alther*
Malice	is like a game of poker or tennis; you don't play it with anyone who is manifestly inferior to you.	*Hilde Spiel*
Manhandle	He took Lenny by the collar, it was like being caught in the slipstream of a jet.	*William McIlvanney*
Manic	as a conquistador with a new world to conquer.	*William McIlvanney*
Many	as crows at a hog-killing.	*Anon.*
Marble	veined and arteried like some living organism.	*Anthony Burgess*
Marriage	is like pleading guilty for an indefinite sentence. Without parole.	*John Mortimer*
Married	Like successful nuns they both had a slightly married air.	*Elizabeth Bowen*
Marrying	is like going bald – there's no parting.	*Anon.*
Matronly	the look of a rather attractive horse matched with the brisk tone of a ward sister.	*John Mortimer*

Maugham (W. Somerset) . . . he looked like the king of the frogs in the fairy tale. With his satiny worn skin he looked as if he was bound in the best quality English calf, you know, the kind of glove leather that doesn't last very long.

Glenway Wescott

Mealy-mouthed as a deacon.   *Anon.*

Mean so mean he'd steal the pennies off a dead man's eyes.

Anon.

Mean so mean he wouldn't pay ten cents to see Christ ride a bicycle up Main Street.   *Anon.*

Meaty as a cucumber sandwich.   *Lindsay Paterson*

Medallion that could have anchored the Queen Mary.

William McIlvanney

Memories My memories are like the coins in the devil's purse: when it was opened nothing was found in it but dead leaves.   *Jean-Paul Sartre*

Men Some men are like musical glasses – to produce their finest tone you must keep them wet.   *S. T. Coleridge*

Men/Women are like buses: there'll be another along soon.   *Anon.*

Middle age is like the second half of a football match.

Beryl Bainbridge

Mind	like a broken cuckoo-clock.	*Martin Amis*

Mind like a steel trap.   *Anon.*

Mind so open that the wind whistles through it.
Heywood Broun

Mind so sharp it could have picnicked on a razor blade.
Richard Brautigan

Mind . . . her sharp mind, sawing raggedly through illusion like a bread knife through a hunk of frozen fish.
Fay Weldon

Mind . . . the mind of the thoroughly well-informed man is a dreadful thing. It is like a bric-a-brac shop, all monsters and dust, with everything priced above its proper value.   *Oscar Wilde*

Mirror with a rounded surface that made me look like a pygmy with water on the brain.   *Raymond Chandler*

Miserable as a horsefly at a dog show.   *Anon.*

Miserable as a rat in a tar-barrel.   *Anon.*

Miserable as a bandicoot.   *Anon. (Australia)*

Miserable as a boil.   *Alida Baxter*

Misleading as last year's map.   *Anon.*

Moan like a she-sheldrake when its mate has had the tip of its wing hurt by a hawk.   *Anon. (Sanskrit)*

Moan like six heifers.   *J. M. Synge*

Modest as a turkey gobbler.   *Ken Kesey*

Mohair sweaters that fluff out like a cat by a project heating duct.
Tom Wolfe

Monarchy is like a splendid ship with all sails set; it moves majestically on, then it hits a rock and sinks forever. Democracy is like a raft. It never sinks, but, damn it, your feet are always in the water.   *Fisher Ames*

Monetarism	is to economics what christian science is to medicine. *Anon.*
Money	is like a sixth sense without which you cannot make a complete use of the other five. *W. Somerset Maugham*
Monotonous	like going to the dentist every day to have the same tooth filled. *Hunter S. Thompson*
Moon	beamed like a junior high school coach. *Ken Kesey*
Moon	The moon was ploughing up the Towy river as if he expected it to yield a crop of stars. *Dylan Thomas*
More	than you could shake a big stick at. *Anon.*
Morecambe pier	like a council house on a stick. *Victoria Wood*
Mousse	. . . the kipper mousse contained more bones than Highgate Cemetery. *Jilly Cooper*
Moustache	one of those moustaches that get stuck under your fingernail. *Raymond Chandler*
Moustache	as thick as jungle foliage. *R. J. Serling*
Mouth	His mouth was foul, as if he had licked rust. *Anon.*
Mouth	like a crack in a pie. *Anon.*

Mouth	like a torn pocket.	*Anon.*
Mouth	like the bottom of a baby's pram – all shit and biscuits.	*Anon.*
Mouth	tasted as if a family of baboons had just moved out.	*Anon.*
Mouth	tasted like a sack full of parrot droppings.	*Anon.*
Mouth	tasted like the bottom of a budgie cage.	*Anon.*
Mouth	a dentist could have got both his hands in, up to the elbows.	*Raymond Chandler*
Mouth	as thin as cigarette paper.	*Raymond Chandler*
Mouth	made for three-decker sandwiches.	*Raymond Chandler*

Mouth	twisted with misery and ham acting.	*Raymond Chandler*
Mouth	felt like an emeritus philologist had curled up and died in it.	*Alan Coren*
Mouth	His multi-hued teeth shone wetly like abandoned tombstones, and his tongue darted in and out of them like a scaly ferret.	*Les Dawson*
Mouth	like a mako shark.	*Clive James*
Mouth	like bent iron.	*Ross Macdonald*

Mouth	like a mail slot.	*Peter de Vries*
Move	slowly and heavily, like a statue thawing reluctantly into flesh.	*Ross Macdonald*
Muesli	like rat droppings in sawdust.	*Jilly Cooper*
Muir (Frank)	[on a motor-scooter] . . . looks like a swan on a piece of cheese.	*Anon.*
Mum	as a sulky crow.	*D. H. Lawrence*
Mumbled	as though his mouth were full of dough.	*Lewis Carroll*
Muscular	as a butcher's pencil.	*Anon.*
Muscular	as dogmeat.	*Rex Beach*
Muscular	built like a dumper truck.	*Tom Davies*

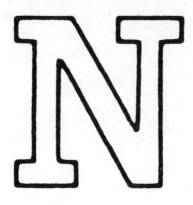

Nagging	like broken teeth.	*Anthony Burgess*
Naked	as Aphrodite fresh from the Aegean.	*Raymond Chandler*
Naked	as an ash tree in the moon of May.	*J. M. Synge*
Nastase (Ilie)	[in defeat] . . . looking like a resigned border-guard who didn't want to cash his opponent's travellers' cheques.	*Julian Barnes*
Nations	The great nations have always acted like gangsters, and the small nations like prostitutes.	*Stanley Kubrick*
Neat	as a knitting pattern.	*Anon.*
Neck	like a Prussian corporal in a cartoon.	*Raymond Chandler*
Need	like a broken neck.	*Anon.*
Need	A woman needs a man like a goldfish needs a motorbike.	*Anon.*
Need	like a tomcat needs a marriage licence.	*Anon. (Ozark – USA)*
Need	like Custer needed more Indians.	*Anon.*
Need	the way William Tell needed a 12-bore.	*Hugh McIlvanney*
Nervous	as a fly in a glue-pot.	*Anon.*
Nervous	strung out like a barrel full of chickens.	*Anon.*
Nervous	like a batsman on ninety-nine.	*Jilly Cooper*
Nervous	as a brick wall.	*Raymond Chandler*
Nervous	as a cricket on a crowded floor.	*Ross Macdonald*

Nervous hilarity of someone who has just run over your cat and hopes to make you see the funny side of it.

Nancy Banks-Smith

New as a new-born newt. *Anon.*

New as the Garden of Eden. *Ross Macdonald*

New as a peeled egg. *Dorothy Parker*

Newspaper The average American newspaper, especially of the so-called better sort, has the intelligence of a Baptist evangelist, the courage of a rat, the fairness of a Prohibitionist boob-bumper, the information of a high-school janitor, the taste of a designer of celluloid valentines and the honour of a police-station lawyer.

H. L. Mencken

Niagara Falls from the air looked like the kitchen sink running over.

Peter de Vries

Nightgown that would turn a monk into Jack the Ripper.

R. J. Sterling

Nipples like hot cherries. *Tom Wolfe*

Nixon (Richard) . . . had the same effect on conservative/Republican politics as Charles Manson and the Hell's Angels had on hippies and flower power. *Hunter S. Thompson*

Nixon (Richard)   . . . the integrity of a hyena and the style of a poison
                       toad.   *Hunter S. Thompson*

Noise   like someone maltreating a pumpkin.   *Ross Macdonald*

Noisy   as a Swiss watch.   *Raymond Chandler*

Nonchalant   as a Red Indian at the stake.   *P. G. Wodehouse*

North sea pipelines   like an upturned plate of spaghetti.   *Eric Varley*

Nose   like a car fender.   *Anon.*

Nose   His nose was particularly white and his large nostrils,
                       correspondingly dark, reminded me of an oboe when
                       they dilated.   *Saul Bellow*

Nose   like a sharp autumn evening, inclined to be frosty
                       towards the end.   *Charles Dickens*

Nose   . . . a classic. It turned up with just the tough tilt of a
                       speedboat planing through the water.   *Norman Mailer*

Nose   Her nose was planted in her face like a knife in an
                       apple.   *Jean-Paul Sartre*

Nose   a fleshy, down-drooping nose like the handle of a
                       derringer.   *Peter de Vries*

Nostrils   wide enough for mouseholes.   *Raymond Chandler*

Novel   Some novels are like soufflés – more notable for their
                       volume than content.   *Anon.*

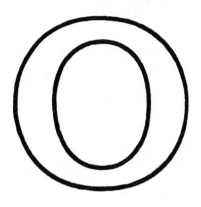

Oblivious	as a mole burrowing a blind path.	*Truman Capote*
Obvious	Her black hair roots showed clear as a patch of acne.	*Anthony Burgess*
Ocean	. . . peaceful and gray, with its lacy edge turned back upon the beach like a chenille bedspread ready for night.	*Ken Kesey*
Ocean	Hung on the horizon like unevenly blued washing.	*Ross Macdonald*
Off	like a big black dog.	*Anon.*
Off	like a bride's nightie.	*Anon.*
Old	so old she's got cobwebs under her arms.	*Anon.*
Old	as Aesop's aunt.	*Raymond Chandler*
Old	like something out of the Book of Revelation.	*Gerald Kersh*
Old gentleman	with the pouched face of a toothless bloodhound and a handshake like a dead fish.	*Gerald Kersh*
Opera	is like a husband with a foreign title: expensive to support, hard to understand and therefore a supreme social challenge.	*Cleveland Amory*
Optimistic	Compared to my mother Micawber looks like Doubting Thomas.	*Alida Baxter*
Organised	. . . could mind mice at a crossroads.	*Patrick Campbell*

Original   all the originality and drive of a split fingernail.
                                                            Raymond Chandler

Originality   as much originality as a Xerox machine.
                                                            Laurence J. Peter

Outnumbered   like having sex with a porcupine: one prick against
                            thousands.   *Wilson Mizner*

Out of place   like an actor who has wandered into the wrong play.
                                                            William McIlvanney

Overgenerous review. . . makes Tennyson's praise of Wellington look like a
                            neck-scissors and body-slam followed by a forearm-
                            smash.   *Martin Amis*

Oxford Station   . . . recently modernised so as to resemble a complex
                            of Wimpy Bars.   *Martin Amis*

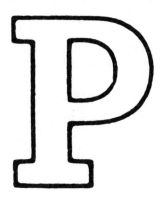

Pale	like Hamlet's father.	*Raymond Chandler*
Pale	like his veins ran skim milk.	*Ken Kesey*
Pale	She had always been as pale as moonlight and had always worn a delicate disdain.	*Dorothy Parker*
Panting	like a method actor finishing a 3.56 mile.	*Tom Wolfe*
Part	as readily as Elastoplast coming off a hairy leg.	*Alida Baxter*
Pathetic	as the violets that bloom on a grave.	*Oscar Wilde*
Patient	as a cigar-store Indian.	*Anon.*
Patiently	as the spider weaves the broken web.	*Bulwer Lytton*
Peace	Fighting for peace is like fornicating for virginity.	*Anon.*

Penicillin   She was pumped so full of penicillin that the fumes
                          from her cured a cold I had.   *Peter de Vries*

Penis   . . . he put it back into his pants as if he were folding
                          a dead octopus tentacle into his shorts.
                                                            Richard Brautigan

Perceptive   not as perceptive as the average tree-stump.
                                                                 Woody Allen

Perceptive   as a one-eyed horse.   *Penry Jones*

Perpendicular   as a poplar.   *Lord Byron*

Persistence   of a pecking gull.   *John Arlott*

Personality   like a rasp.   *Anon.*

Phone   started to ring like an aural booby trap. *Ross Macdonald*

Phoney   as the pedigree of a used car.   *Raymond Chandler*

Photographer   is like the cod, which produces a million eggs in order
                          that one may reach maturity.   *George Bernard Shaw*

Pink   as a spanked baby's ass.   *Anon. (Ozark – USA)*

Plain   as a barn door.   *Anon.*

Platinumed hair   . . . so her head shone like a silver fruit-bowl.
                                                            Raymond Chandler

Playboy   A woman reading *Playboy* feels a little like a Jew
                          reading a Nazi manual.   *Gloria Steinem*

Pleasant	as a boil on the sphincter.	*William McIlvanney*
Pleased	as a dog with two tails.	*Anon.*
Pleased	as if he'd just brought the good news from Ghent to Aix.	*William McIlvanney*
Pleasurable	as your chin after a barber's shop shave.	*Alan White*
Plump	as a miller's sparrow.	*Anon.*
Point	as elusive as the needle's in the haystack.	*Richard Gordon*
Pointless	as if a car had crashed, the driver was dead and the radio still played to him.	*William McIlvanney*
Polished	as a mart-day pig.	*Lewis Grassic Gibbon*
Politicians	like the earth, are flattened at the polls.	*Anon.*
Politics	is like boxing – you try to knock out your opponent.	*Idi Amin*
Polls	are like bikinis; what they reveal is interesting, but what they conceal is vital.	*Len Murray*
Pompous	He spoke as if every word would lift a dish.	*Anon.*

Poor	as Job's turkey.	*Ross Macdonald*
Popular	as a pork chop in a synagogue.	*Anon.*

Popular	as an armed and uniformed invader. *Patrick Campbell*
Popular	as eating live goldfish. *Hunter S. Thompson*
Popular	as Public Enemy Number One at the annual Policemen's Ball. *P. G. Wodehouse*
Pornographic films	Nipples cover the screen like acne on a juvenile's forehead. *Stephen Pile*
Pose	putting up her face like a duck to the moon. *Joyce Cary*
Pounce	He rushed . . . into the bedroom and pounced on her like a bird-eating spider. *Gerald Kersh*
Pouting	as if she was extinguishing a delicate candle. *William McIlvanney*
Powerless	as a blind kitten in a bucket of water. *Walter Greenwood*
Practical	as dusting the coals. *Gerald Kersh*
Precision	the awesome precision of a fighter pilot swatting flies. *Clive James*
Pretend	like a man shaping up to his mirror. *William McIlvanney*
Pretending	There are fascists pretending to be humanitarians like cannibals on a health kick eating only vegetarians. *Roger McGough*
Pretty	as a gargoyle. *Anon.*
Pretty	as a lily on a dungpile. *Anon.*
Pretty	as a mud flat. *Anon.*
Pretty	as a new-laid egg. *Anon. (Ozark – USA)*
Primitive	. . . life forms so amazingly primitive that they still think digital watches are a pretty neat idea. *Douglas Adams*

Prince Charles	In presenting press awards I feel rather like a pheasant giving out prizes to the best shots.	
		Charles, Prince of Wales
Pristine	as discarded tissue paper.	*Anon.*
Private	as a toothbrush.	*O. Henry*
Profile	like a chicken's.	*Kingsley Amis*
Promiscuous	had seen more pricks than a second-hand dart board.	*Anon.*
Protective	like feeling protective towards *HMS Hood* or Mick McManus.	*Jan Webster*
Proud	as a tom-tit on a horse turd.	*Anon.*
Publicity	. . . eats publicity like I eat tender young garden peas.	*Raymond Chandler*
Punch	like being hit on the jaw with the back of a shovel.	*William McIlvanney*
Punk	[in black leather] like a puffin in an oil slick.	*Janey Preger*
Punk music	burst on the music scene like a boil.	*Anon.*

Puppy   . . . a cock like a radish.   *Craig Raine*

Pure   I'm as pure as the driven slush.   *Tallulah Bankhead*

Question	like the question of the authorship of the *Iliad* . . . either Homer, or, if not Homer, somebody else of the same name.	*Aldous Huxley*
Queue	moved forward slowly like a coloured snake drunk with sun.	*Ross Macdonald*
Quick	as a nun's kiss.	*Anon.*
Quick	as a rat up a drainpipe.	*Anon.*
Quick	as a snake through a hollow log.	*Anon. (Ozark – USA)*
Quick	as a yaller dog running downhill.	*Anon. (USA)*
Quick	as a trout up a burn.	*Bill McLaren*
Quicker	than hell would scorch a feather.	*Anon.*
Quiescent	London is restful, as quiescent as a dinner with JPs.	*D. H. Lawrence*
Quiet	as a clockwork canary.	*Anon.*
Quiet	as a locked door.	*Anon.*
Quiet	as a wasp in one's nose.	*Anon.*
Quiet	as a Celtic supporter at the Rangers end.	*Anon. (Glasgow)*
Quiet	as a spider attaching its thread.	*Honoré de Balzac*
Quiet	as a mousehole.	*Anon.*

99

Quiet   such a quiet you could near have cut it and eaten it in
                         chunks.   *Lewis Grassic Gibbon*

Quiet   It was that quiet you could hear the snails breathing.
                                                               William McIlvanney

Quiet   so quiet you could hear a rat piss on cotton.
                                                                    Norma Miller

Quivering   like a virgin's fan.   *G. MacDonald Fraser*

Quizzical   She looks at me as if I am a foreign movie that has
                         just come in out of the snow starring Jean-Paul
                         Belmondo and Catherine Deneuve.   *Richard Brautigan*

Quizzical   like someone smiling with a mouthful of salts.
                                                             G. MacDonald Fraser

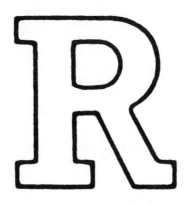

Rabbit legs	Surrounded with cold white fat, they looked like maps of Greenland and tasted like a dryad's inner thigh. *Clive James*
Rain	pouring fit to frighten Noah. *G. MacDonald Fraser*
Rain	like a cow wettin' on a flat rock. *Anon.*
Rain	was rustling like Cellophane at the window. *Ross Macdonald*
Rapt expression	like a hunky immigrant looking at the Statue of Liberty. *Raymond Chandler*
Rare	as gold on the beach. *Anon.*
Rare	as rich uncles. *Anon.*
Rare	as rocking-horse shit. *Anon.*
Rare	as virgins in Paris. *Anon.*
Rare	as hairy, spotted elephants. *Patrick Campbell*
Rare	as a pink zebra. *Raymond Chandler*
Rash	had the look of angry oatmeal. *Anthony Burgess*
Rash	like challenging a school of piranhas to a game of water polo. *Thomas H. Middleton*
Raw	as broken eggs. *Anon.*
React	the way a stuffed fish reacts to bait. *Raymond Chandler*
Read	solemnly, like a man with the Elgin marbles in his mouth. *Dylan Thomas*

101

Reagan (Ronald)	. . . a face like an aubergine in a string bag.	*Anon.*
Reassuring	as a dentist with an instruction manual.	*Anon.*
Recoil	from it as if it were the hand of a drowning man clutching at him.	*William McIlvanney*
Redundant	like a gunfighter pitted against germ warfare.	*William McIlvanney*

Reformer	like a guy who rides through a sewer in a glass-bottomed boat.	*James J. Walker*
Regular	as mother's phone calls.	*Anon.*
Relevant	as brushing a corpse's teeth.	*William McIlvanney*
Reliable	as the weather during a Test Match.	*Anon.*
Relieved	. . . the look of the man against the wall bravely refusing the eye-bandage and last cigarette, noticing a bloke on a horse galloping over the horizon waving a bit of paper explaining the verdict was all a ghastly mistake.	*Richard Gordon*
Relish	like a domestic servant proclaiming a catastrophe.	*Saki*
Responsive	as a sarcophagus.	*Alida Baxter*
Restful	as a split lip.	*Anon.*
Restful	as the charge of the Light Brigade.	*Anon.*
Restless	as a one-armed paper hanger with crabs.	*Anon.*
Restless	as the tip of a cat's tail.	*Anon.*

Restless	as fleas.	*Raymond Chandler*
Rich	like a bouncer who had come into money.	*Raymond Chandler*
Rich	. . . he got richer quicker than the only sober man in a poker game.	*G. MacDonald Fraser*
Rich	as creosote.	*P. G. Wodehouse*
Richer	than six feet down in Iowa.	*Damon Runyon*
Ride	like a hog on a hurdle.	*Anon.*
Ring	Her ringed hand turned like a lighthouse.	*William McIlvanney*
River	Metallic . . . like an aluminium rainbow, like a slice of alloy moon.	*Ken Kesey*
Road	looked like a seal's back in the rain.	*Dashiell Hammett*
Road (to the sea)	straight as a herd of lemmings.	*Tove Jansson*
Roar	like a bull in torment.	*George Mackay Brown*
Robust	as rice pudding.	*Tom Wolfe*
Romantic	as Adolf Hitler.	*Ed McBain*
Rooting	like a pig on a truffle run.	*Patrick Campbell*
Rotten (Johnny)	. . . a cuttlefish in human form.	*Clive James*

Rough	as a goat's knee.	*Anon.*
Rough	as a rat catcher's dog.	*Anon.*
Rough	as bags.	*Anon. (Australia)*
Round	as a Pontypool waiter.	*Anon.*
Row brewing	like a constipated storm-cloud, the sulphurous tonnage of words built up unsaid.	*Alida Baxter*
Run	like Groucho Marx stalking a waitress.	*John Arlott*
Running round	like Chicken Little with her head chopped off.	*Ken Kesey*
Russell (Bertrand)	like a sleepy eagle nestling into his father's clothes.	*Alistair Cooke*

| Sad | as hi-jinks in an invaded land. | *Nelson Algren* |

Sad as hi-jinks in an invaded land. *Nelson Algren*

Safe as a church tied to a hedge. *Anon.*

Safe as a crow in a gutter. *Anon.*

Safe as a mouse in a malt heap. *Anon.*

Sag like a fisherman's hat. *Irvin S. Cobb*

Saggy as a sponge full of treacle. *Angus McNeill*

Sales a sales graph like an extremely dangerous ski-slope. *Anon.*

Sane as a Scots nanny. *John Pepper*

Scan the room like Wild Bill Hickock entering the Crazy Legs Saloon. *Tom Wolfe*

Scarce as Len's teeth. *Anon. (Australia)*

Scarce as the cardinal virtues. *Ross Macdonald*

Scared as a turkey in November. *Anon.*

Scarf you could have found in the dark by listening to it purr. *Raymond Chandler*

Scilly Isles Out there, like seal and pouting puffin
The people live right next to nuffin. *Leslie Thomas*

Scottish drunks Whereas English drunks tend to shamble along,
Scottish drunks perform a strange twitching dance,
like laboratory frogs wired up to the mains.
Simon Hoggart

Scream   like a guinea hen just worked over by a pack of wild
                    dogs.   *Hunter S. Thompson*

Screech   like fingernails across a blackboard.   *Anon.*

Seagulls   wheeling like a complex mobile suspended from the
                    sky.   *Ross Macdonald*

Seasoned   as highly seasoned as a tongue depressor.
                                                             Ross Macdonald

Secret   as well kept a secret as the real colour of Ronald
                    Reagan's hair.   *Primrose Milligan*

Secret   like something lovely and fragrant laid away in
                    lavender.   *P. G. Wodehouse*

Self-confidence of a rabbit with a retiring disposition caught in the
                    headlights of an oncoming car.   *John Mortimer*

Senility   . . . the wires of the cerebral cortex hang in the skull
                    like a clump of dried seaweed.   *Tom Wolfe*

Sense   as much sense as God gave to geese.   *Anon.*

Sense of duty   like a National Health prostitute.   *Roger McGough*

Sensible   as worrying in case, next Christmas, the giant catches
                    Jack before he gets down the beanstalk.   *Roy Hattersley*

Sensible	as trying out a new ballet at the Aldershot Garrison Theatre. *Frank Muir*
Sensitive	as cement. *Anon.*
Sensitive	as a fag end in a docker's navel. *Roger McGough*
Sensitive	as a goddam toilet seat. *J. D. Salinger*
Sensitivity	the delicate sensitivity of a frightened rattlesnake. *Ross Macdonald*
Sermons	were like students' songs imperfectly recalled by a senile don. *John Rae*
Set in his ways	as a street car. *David Niven*

Sex	like having a beautiful picnic in a field of comets. *Richard Brautigan*
Sex appeal	as much sex appeal as a road accident. *Douglas Adams*
Sex censorship	. . . the British Board of Censors will not pass any seduction scene unless the seducer has one foot on the floor. Apparently sex in England is something like snooker. *Fred Allen*

Sexless	as a schoolboy, she looked into the future.	
		Margaret Kennedy
Sexual activity	like a pig's tail; going all day and nothing done at night.	*Anon.*
Sexy	as a bag of chips.	*Anon.*
Sexy	as a side of bacon in deep freeze.	*Les Dawson*
Sexy	as the General Council of the TUC.	*Denis Norden*
Sexy	as a vandalised launderama.	*Victoria Wood*
Shake	like the lead singer in a rumba band.	*Woody Allen*
Shame	as if he had shot a beater.	*Graham Greene*
Sharp	as a box of ferrets.	*Anon.*
Sharp	as a ferret at a field-rat's hole.	*Anon.*
Sharp	as a pound of margarine.	*Anon.*
Sharp	as a wet Kleenex.	*Anon.*
Sharp	as frost.	*Anon.*
Sharp	as a cracker and twice as crumby.	*Anon. (California)*
Shifty	as a shithouse rat.	*Anon.*
Shine	like a diamond on a dead man's hand.	*Anon.*
Shine	like the seat of a bus driver's trousers.	*P. G. Wodehouse*
Ship	like a floating soap dish.	*Richard Gordon*
Shirt	like a nasty accident with a school dinner.	
		Victoria Wood
Shiver	like a sick child in a cold cradle.	*Charlotte Brontë*
Shocked	like a man who, chasing rainbows, has one of them suddenly turn and bite him in the leg.	
		P. G. Wodehouse

Shoes	Englishwomen's shoes look as if they had been made by someone who had often heard shoes described, but had never seen any. *Margaret Halsey*

Shoes	Moving, the shoes made a noise like cow pats at the moment of impact. *Clive James*
Shoes	the size of Volkswagens. *Clive James*
Shoes	Garbo's feet were beautifully shaped and long . . . but she had an unfortunate habit of encasing them in huge brown 'loafers' which gave the impression that she wore landing craft. *David Niven*
Shop steward	is a little like an egg. If you keep him in hot water long enough he gets hard boiled. *Jack Tanner*
Short	as a British summer. *Anon.*
Short and sweet	like a donkey's gallop. *Anon.*
Shorter	than a bargain counter shirt. *Raymond Chandler*
Shoulders	. . . sports coat not wider at the shoulders than a two-car garage. *Raymond Chandler*
Shoulders	like frying chickens'. *Ross Macdonald*
Shrill	as a dog whistle. *Anon.*
Shrill	like a chicken in a frenzy. *Joseph Heller*
Shrivel	like a jellyfish in the sun. *George Mackay Brown*

Shrivelled	. . . small, shrivelled chap. Looks like a haddock with lung trouble.	*P. G. Wodehouse*
Shrivelled	like a Peruvian shrunken head.	*Tom Wolfe*
Shuddering	like gourmets who had blundered into a Mexican taco shop.	*S. J. Perelman*
Shuffle	like a Sumo wrestler waiting for the decision.	*G. Talese*
Shut up	like a telescope.	*Lewis Carroll*
Shy	and sensitive as a seismograph.	*David Niven*
Sick	as mud.	*P. G. Wodehouse*
Sick	feeling more or less like something the Pure Food Committee had rejected.	*P. G. Wodehouse*
Sigh	a big sigh, like a burst tyre.	*Joyce Cary*
Sigh	a dejected sigh like a cake falling.	*Ken Kesey*
Sightless	as marbles.	*Raymond Chandler*
Significant	as a piss in Niagara Falls.	*Anon.*
Silence	sounded as if a machine had broken down.	*Richard Brautigan*
Silence	as heavy as a waterlogged boat.	*Raymond Chandler*
Silence	fell like a bag of feathers.	*Raymond Chandler*
Silence	ran between them like a fuse.	*William McIlvanney*
Silent	as the 'p' in swimming.	*Anon.*
Silent	He hands out words like Masonic secrets.	*Peter MacDougall*
Silently	as a snake sloughing off its skin.	*Patrick Campbell*
Silly	as a two bob watch.	*Anon.*
Similes	are like songs of love They much describe; they nothing prove.	*Matthew Prior*

Similes	in each dull line like glowworms in the dark should shine. *Edward Moore*
Simple	eyes as simple as forest water. *Raymond Chandler*
Sincerity	as luminous as a halo. *Patrick Campbell*
Sincerity	all the sincerity of a boa constrictor contemplating his next meal. *Lord Cudlipp*
Sincerity	in society . . . [is] like an iron girder in a house of cards. *W. Somerset Maugham*
Sing	like four canaries and a steel guitar. *Raymond Chandler*
Singing	like a cat screaming with the anguish of a strangled hernia. The veins on her neck resembled rhubarb stalks as she strained like a hen laying a triangular egg. *Les Dawson*
Sipping (drink)	with carefree enjoyment, rather like Caesar having one in his tent the day he overcame the Nervii. *P. G. Wodehouse*
Sit	like a toad on a shovel. *Anon.*
Sit down	I dropped like dung into the nearest chair. *Peter de Vries*
Sit down	. . . settle at a table like a carthorse backing into the shafts. *Jan Webster*

Skin   as mottled as a tablecloth in a cheap cafeteria.

Groucho Marx

Skin   Your skin is like a Fair Isle sweater. . . . And like a
                Fair Isle sweater, it is a living, breathing thing full of
                natural oils.   *Frank Muir*

Skin   like the petals of wood anemones.   *Dorothy Parker*

Skin   as thin as bromo.   *Evelyn Waugh*

Sky   was like washed-out Jap silk and there were just a few
                little clouds coming out of it like down feathers out of
                an old cushion.   *Joyce Cary*

Slacks   . . . packed into her slacks like two big scoops of
                vanilla ice cream.   *Woody Allen*

Sleek   as seals.   *Tove Jansson*

Sleep   like dead meat.   *Anthony Burgess*

Sleep   Mr and Mrs Floyd, the cocklers, are sleeping as quiet
                as death, side by wrinkled side, toothless salt and
                brown, like two old kippers in a box.   *Dylan Thomas*

Sleeping   like a photograph.   *Richard Brautigan*

Slick   as a sonnet.   *Anon.*

Slide   like a snail over a bald head.   *Anon.*

Slim	as a bluebell.	*John Mortimer*
Slip away	like a knotless thread.	*Anon.*
Slippery	The deck was as slippery as greased owlshit.	*Anon. (oil-rig worker)*
Slow	as smoke off a dung pile.	*Anon. (Ozark – USA)*
Slow	as the Tweed comes to Melrose.	*Anon. (Scots)*
Slow	as Christmas.	*Ken Kesey*
Small	so small he broke his leg falling off the kerb.	*Anon.*
Small	so small he bust his lip on the kerb.	*Anon.*
Small	so small he can sit on a cigarette paper and hang his feet over the edge.	*Anon.*
Small	so small you'd need a step ladder to put your shoes on.	*Raymond Chandler*
Smarm	like a fart-licking spaniel.	*Dylan Thomas*
Smart	as a new-scraped carrot.	*Anon.*
Smart	as a whip.	*Anon.*
Smart	like a smacked bottom.	*Anon.*
Smart	as a brilliantined trout.	*Dylan Thomas*

Smell	higher than lobster bait.	*Anon.*
Smell	like a lodging house cat.	*Anon.*
Smell	goes round your heart like a hairy worm.	*Anon. (Aberdeen)*
Smell	like a thousand tomcats had been shut in all night.	*George Mackay Brown*
Smell	A cheesey smell of curds rose to meet him like a small grey spirit.	*Anthony Burgess*
Smell	strong enough to build a garage on.	*Raymond Chandler*
Smell	like a tart's window box.	*Anon.*
Smell	I was certain I smelled better than Hot Cakes Rabinowitz. It would have been difficult to smell worse.	*Jerome Weidman*
Smelly	as a gorilla's armpit.	*Anon.*
Smile	like winter sunshine glinting on a coffin lid.	*Anon.*
Smile	like a girl in a garden.	*George Mackay Brown*
Smile	He turned it off at once like testing a torch battery.	*Anthony Burgess*
Smile	a brilliant warm smile, like the kiss of death.	*Raymond Chandler*
Smile	a nice smile, like an alligator.	*Raymond Chandler*
Smile	of a man whose mind is not smiling.	*Raymond Chandler*
Smile	She gave me a smile I could feel in my hip-pocket.	*Raymond Chandler*
Smile	the kind of smile that goes with a silk noose.	*Raymond Chandler*
Smile	as brittle as a dried chicken bone.	*Jilly Cooper*

Smile (J.R.'s)	like a greedy amorous cuttlefish, a set of teeth mounted on a large need. *Stanley Eveling*

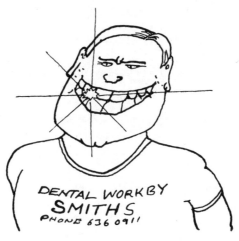

Smile	like a happy crocodile's. *G. MacDonald Fraser*
Smile	a smile plucked out like a last swede plucked from a frozen field. *Lewis Grassic Gibbon*
Smile	resembled the painful reopening of a wound. *Graham Greene*
Smile	like a Pacific sunrise. *Barry Humphries*
Smile	like a broken clay dish. *Ken Kesey*
Smile	like a corpse in a deft mortician's hands. *Ross Macdonald*
Smile	as wide as his wallet. *William McIlvanney*
Smile	like a Christmas tree. *William McIlvanney*
Smile	the kind of smile a victorious boxer gives the loser. *William McIlvanney*
Smile	curved like a banana. *Albert Morris*
Smile	like the cracking of frozen leather. *R. J. Serling*

Smile	combines James Dean, Porfiro Rubirosa and a teenage bank clerk with a foolproof embezzlement scheme.	*Hunter S. Thompson*
Smile	A smile split her face like a coconut.	*Peter de Vries*
Smile	the kind of smile with which money is cheerfully refunded.	*Peter de Vries*
Smile	the sort of weak smile Roman gladiators used to give the Emperor before entering the arena.	*P. G. Wodehouse*
Smiling	encouragement, like a clumsy dentist.	*Katherine Mansfield*
Smoke	hanging in the air like lazing ghosts.	*Tom Davies*
Smoking	like a smouldering mattress.	*Joseph Heller*
Smooth	as a baby's bottom by moonlight.	*Anon.*
Smooth	as a bandleader's hair.	*Raymond Chandler*
Smooth	as an angel's wing.	*Raymond Chandler*
Smooth	as a prune.	*Raymond Chandler*
Smoothly	as a pig on stilts.	*Anon.*
Smug	as a canary-swallowing cat.	*David Niven*
Snappy	as an elastic band.	*Jilly Cooper*
Sniff	like a dredger.	*Alida Baxter*
Snore	like a pig in the sun.	*Anon.*
Snow	sounds as if someone was kissing the window all over outside.	*Lewis Carroll*
Snow	crackles underfoot like powdered bones.	*Roger McGough*
Snowflakes	like small doilies.	*Peter de Vries*

Snug	as safe and snug as a bugger in Rugby.	*Dylan Thomas*
Sober	as a judge on Friday.	*Anon.*
Sober	as some judges.	*Damon Runyon*

Socially acceptable	. . . more socially acceptable than pulling a halibut from under your jacket.	*Woody Allen*
Soft	as a South wind.	*Anon.*
Soft	as suet.	*Anon.*
Soft	as primroses.	*Jilly Cooper*
Soft	enough to put a finger through.	*Ross Macdonald*
Soft	as an uncut diamond.	*Ed McBain*
Soft	A soft lad the like of you wouldn't slit the wind pipe of a screeching sow.	*J. M. Synge*
Soothing	and empty as cows' eyes.	*Anthony Burgess*
Sore	as a mashed thumb.	*Irvin S. Cobb*
Sore	as a sunburned neck.	*P. G. Wodehouse*
Sore	as a gumboil.	*Anon.*
Soufflé	looking like a diseased custard.	*P. G. Wodehouse*
Sound	as a trout.	*Anon.*
Sour	so sour you could make yoghurt out of him.	*Jilly Cooper*

Sour   looks as if he had been weaned on a pickle.
                                                Alice Roosevelt-Longworth

Spattered   Lightning spattered the sky like a thrown egg on a
                        barn door.   *Rudyard Kipling*

Speak   like a mouse in a cheese.   *Anon.*

Speak   as if her throat were lined with silk and satin and she
                        had a tulip for a tongue.   *George Mackay Brown*

Speak   He gave him the word as if it came out of a blowpipe.
                                                        William McIlvanney

Speak   As if coated with grease, words slid from his great
                        lips, and his tones were those of one who cozens the
                        sick.   *Dorothy Parker*

Speak   She smacked the word as if it had been delicious with
                        salt and onion.   *Dorothy Parker*

Speak   sweet as a razor.   *Dylan Thomas*

Spectacular   like watching a drunk run through traffic on a
                        freeway.   *Hunter S. Thompson*

Speechless   My vocal cords, anyway, seemed stuck together like
                        strands of over-cooked spaghetti.   *Saul Bellow*

Speed   and reactions of a striking slug.   *Anon.*

Spend	He threw his money about like a man with no arms. *William McIlvanney*
Split	like a mule kicking a watermelon. *Ken Kesey*
Sport and politics	Saying sport and politics don't mix is like a milkman watching someone put a bomb on his float, ignoring it because it's nothing to do with him, and driving up to the woman and kiddies at the next house. *Hugh McIlvanney*
Sports club dance	Not so much a dance, really, more a game of water polo played in spilled beer. *Alida Baxter*
Spot	like a surgically implanted walnut. *Martin Amis*
Spotted	like an exotic acne. *William McIlvanney*
Spout	like a hog in a bucket of slops. *Nelson Algred*
Sprawl	like drunken cattle rustlers in a B film. *Alistair Cooke*
Sprawl	like a starfish of the genus Echinodermata. *S. J. Perelman*
Squeak	. . . squeaking and gibbering like the sheeted dead in the Roman streets a little ere the mightiest Julius fell. *P. G. Wodehouse*
Squeal	like a pig with his head caught in a slop bucket. *Woody Guthrie*
Stagger	like a manic Max Wall. *Jan Webster*
Stamina	like a brewery horse. *Harpo Marx*
Stand out	like a dog's balls. *Anon.*
Stand out	so far you could break off a yard of it and still have enough for a baseball bat. *Raymond Chandler*
Stand out	like a chicken hawk in a flock of pullets. *Ross Macdonald*
Stand out	like a dead fly in a bowl of cream. *Walter J. Millar*

Stand out	like a wicked fairy at a christening. *Anon.*
Stand out	like a nudist at a winter sports resort. *William McIlvanney*
Stare	The fixed expressions of rabbits on a night road who think that the best way of dealing with approaching headlights is to stare them out. *Douglas Adams*
Stare	like a choked thrush. *Anon.*
Stare	like a rather blotto tourist seeing a swell sunset on Mount Whitney. *Raymond Chandler*
Stars	like fire engines hanging in the air and streams of light coming from their hoses. *Richard Brautigan*
Start	like a nymph surprised while bathing. *P. G. Wodehouse*
Statistics	can be employed like a drunk uses a lamp post – for support rather than illumination. *Anon.*
Steady	as a stone pier in a light breeze. *Raymond Chandler*
Steak	like *Gone With The Wind*. *Alida Baxter*
Stealthy	as an iguana. *Roger McGough*
Stern	a face like a well-kept grave. *Anon.*

Stewart (Rod)	Wearing very tight striped pants, he looked like a bifurcated marrow . . . like a pensionable cherub.	*Clive James*
Stick	like shit to a blanket.	*Anon.*
Stick	like a tick in a hound dog's ear.	*Anon. (USA)*
Stick out	like a trumpet in the violins.	*Joyce Cary*
Stick out	like spats at an Iowa picnic.	*Raymond Chandler*
Stick together	like a bag of humbugs.	*Anon.*
Stiff	as a five-day corpse.	*Anon.*
Stiff	as a frozen fish.	*Raymond Chandler*

Stiff	as a wax dummy.	*Raymond Chandler*
Still	as the pennies on a dead man's eyes.	*Anon.*
Still	so still you could hear a cricket clear his throat.	*Anon. (Ozark – USA)*
Still	as fallen leaves.	*Sean O'Faolain*
Stocky	built short and up from the bottom like a fire hydrant.	*Tom Wolfe*
Straight	as a beggar can spit.	*Anon.*
Straight	as a pound of candles.	*Anon.*

Straight   as a yard of pump water.   *Anon.*

Straight   as a stale banana.   *Raymond Chandler*

Straight   as a trombone slide.   *Dudley Doust*

Straighter   than a preacher's dream.   *Woody Guthrie*

Strain   like a gravel truck on a hairpin turn. *Raymond Chandler*

Streets   white and dry like a collision at a high rate of speed
                        between a cemetery and a truck loaded with sacks of
                        flour.   *Richard Brautigan*

Strong   as father's socks.   *Anon.*

Struggle   like an alligator in a handbag factory.   *Anon.*

Struggle on   like a candle guttering and clinging in a draught.
                                                                  D. H. Lawrence

Strut   like a crow in a gutter.   *Anon.*

Strut   like an old dog in the May moon.   *Joyce Cary*

Stunned   as though she had been hit with a halibut.
                                                                   David Niven

Style   and grace of an ice floe in the North Atlantic.
                                                             Hunter S. Thompson

Suave   as a row of head waiters.   *Barry Took*

Subtle	as an avalanche.	*Anon.*
Subtle	as a mugging.	*Anon.*
Subtle	as an enraged dinosaur.	*Anon.*
Subtle	as Coventry cathedral.	*Anon.*

Subtle	as a steam roller in overdrive.	*Jilly Cooper*
Succeed	as unlikely to succeed as a ballet dancer with a wooden leg.	*Raymond Chandler*
Success	Moderation is a fatal thing. . . . Nothing succeeds like excess.	*Oscar Wilde*
Suggest	like a doctor to a dithering hypochondriac.	*Alistair Cooke*
Sun	The sun was like a huge fifty-cent piece that someone had poured kerosene on and then had lit with a match and said, 'Here, hold this while I go get a newspaper,' and put the coin in my hand, but never came back.	*Richard Brautigan*
Sun	that would melt a man's eye like butter did he not wink.	*Anthony Burgess*
Sun	. . . in a mist. Like an orange in a fried-fish shop.	*Joyce Cary*
Sun	the colourless sun only just visible through the grey clouds, like an empty plate on a dirty tablecloth.	*Len Deighton*

Sun	like a sallow lemon.	*Stella Gibbons*

Sun   hit me smartly on the face, like a bully.   *Laurie Lee*

Sun   a Glasgow sun, dully luminous, an eye with cataract.
                                                   William McIlvanney

Sun   In a shuttered room I roast
             Like a pumpkin in a serra.
             And the sun like buttered toast
             Drips upon the classic terra. *Dylan Thomas (in Florence)*

Sun   beaming like a cheap salesman.   *Leslie Thomas*

Sun   is plugged in up there like God's own dentist lamp.
                                                            Tom Wolfe

Sunburned   like a neon radish.   *Paul Kerton*

Sunflower   as big as a four-passenger omelette.   *W. Pegler*

Sunlight   tarnished as a Spanish coin.   *Ed McBain*

Sunshine   as strong as a blow in the chops.   *Anthony Burgess*

Superficial all the depth and glitter of a worn dime.
                                                       Dorothy Parker

Sure   as death and taxes.   *Anon.*

Sure   as a dead man stinks.   *Anon. (Ozark – USA)*

Sure   as snakes crawl.   *Anon. (Ozark – USA)*

Surely   as a blind man's dog pulls him into a butcher's shop.
                                                     Maurice Hewlett

Surprise   . . . looked at me as if I had just come up from the
             floor of the ocean with a drowned mermaid under my
             arm.   *Raymond Chandler*

Surprise   Their eyes swelled up like young grapefruits.
                                                   Hunter S. Thompson

Surprise   like . . . one who, picking daisies on the railway, has
             just caught the down express in the small of the back.
                                                      P. G. Wodehouse

Surprised	as if he'd been asked for a lightly grilled stoat in a bun with French fries. *Douglas Adams*
Surprised look	like a poleaxed lamb in that wobbly moment just before the cerebral cortex shuts off for good. *Tom Wolfe*
Surprise find	as if the janitor had gone out to buy a tin of paint and had returned with a Velasquez. *David Lacey*
Survive	as fitted to survive as a tapeworm in an intestine. *William Golding*
Suspicious	It stank like a dead camel. *G. MacDonald Fraser*
Swallow	convulsively, like a Pekingese taking a pill. *P. G. Wodehouse*
Swear	like a pirate's parrot. *Gavin Lyall*
Sweat	gathering in his eyebrows like dew in a thicket. *Ross Macdonald*
Sweet	as a honey bear's tooth. *Anon.*
Sweet	so sweet you could eat her with a spoon. *S. J. Perelman*

Swimming pool   about the size of Lake Huron but a lot neater.
                                                           Raymond Chandler

Sympathy   as much sympathy as a lone shark.   *Raymond Chandler*

Sympathy   like a machine gun riddling her hostess with
                         sympathy.   *Aldous Huxley*

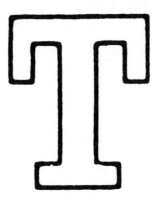

Tables (restaurant)	the size of throat lozenges.	*Peter de Vries*
Tact	all the tact and discretion of a lobotomised orang-utang which has just sat on a hedgehog.	*Martin Amis*
Take to	like a Scotsman to drink.	*Anon.*
Talk	like a recently released Trappist.	*Michael Bentine*
Talk	with all the verve and panache of a speaking clock.	*Clement Freud*
Talk	which might be likened to footprints, so strong and definite was the impression which it left behind.	*Mark Twain*
Talkative	. . . a mouth so loose it was surprising his teeth stayed in.	*William McIlvanney*
Talkative	like a book without covers.	*William McIlvanney*
Tame	as a kitchen cat on a houseboat.	*Anon.*
Tantalising	like smelling whiskey through a jail house window.	*Anon. (Ozark – USA)*
Taste	like a cholera culture.	*Raymond Chandler*
Taste	like a plumber's handkerchief.	*Raymond Chandler*
Tasteful	as that statuette of the Milo Venus with the clock in her stomach.	*Dorothy Parker*
Tasteless	as a roadhouse blonde.	*Raymond Chandler*
Tax	My tax is high as an elephant's eye.	*Groucho Marx*

Tea   like warm battery fluid.   *Albert Morris*

Teamwork   as much idea of teamwork as Georgie Best.
                                                   Army TV commercial

Tears   fell like millstones.   *William McIlvanney*

Teeth   . . . jangling in his head, like a pocketful of loose
                       change.   *Martin Amis*

Teeth   like serried snow-gems.   *Anthony Burgess*

Teeth   . . . a row of fashionably neglected teeth lovely as
                       datestones.   *Alan Coren*

Teeth   like the pieces of broken glass people put on their
                       walls.   *Edmond and Jules de Goncourt*

Teeth   like a spider with a mouthful of pins.   *Gerald Kersh*

Teeth   His front teeth glared at me like a pair of chisels.
                                                         Ross Macdonald

Teeth   like a row of icicles.   *William McIlvanney*

Teeth   like the Ten Commandments, all broken.
                                                    Herbert Beerbohm Tree

Teeth brace   a smile that looked like a car crash.   *Clive James*

Tentative   as a bird.   *Anon.*

Thatcher (Margaret)   sounded like a cat sliding down a blackboard.
                                                            Clive James

Thatcher (Margaret)	has done for monetarism what the Boston Strangler did for door-to-door salesmen. *Denis Healey*
Theatre	a tawdry affair, all Cupids and cornucopias, like a third-rate wedding-cake. *Oscar Wilde*
Theologian	like a blind man in a dark room searching for a black cat which isn't there – and finding it! *Anon.*
Thick	as a tin of paint. *Anon.*
Thick	as mince. *Anon.*
Thick	as shit in the neck of a bottle. *Anon.*
Thick	as two mongrel puppies. *Anon.*
Thick	as two short planks. *Anon.*
Thick	as two body snatchers. *O Henry*
Thin	as a hoofer's wallet. *Raymond Chandler*
Thin	as an honest alibi. *Raymond Chandler*
Thin	as the homeopathic soup that was made by boiling the shadow of a pigeon that had been starved to death. *Abraham Lincoln*
Thin	as the husks of insects after spiders had eaten them. *Ross Macdonald*
Thinner	than the gold on a weekend wedding ring. *Raymond Chandler*
Thirst	so great it would throw a shadow. *Hunter S. Thompson*

Thirsty	. . . throat feels like a leper's armpit.	*Alexander Frater*
Threadbare	as a book-keeper's coat.	*Raymond Chandler*
Threat	rather like threatening me with being banned from Woolworths.	*Nigel Dempster*
Thrilled	quivered like a mousse.	*P. G. Wodehouse*
Throat	the kind of throat that would have looked better in a football sweater.	*Raymond Chandler*
Thrust	aside like a curtain.	*Anthony Burgess*
Thumbnail	like the blade of a shovel.	*Anon.*
Tidy	as a fresh-veiled nun.	*Honoré de Balzac*
Tight	as a duck's bum.	*Anon.*
Tight	as a gnat's chuff.	*Anon.*
Tight	as a mouse's ear.	*Anon.*
Tight	as a fat lady's girdle.	*Raymond Chandler*
Tight	He's so tight his head squeaks when he takes his hat off.	*Raymond Chandler*
Time	less time than it takes to say 'God' with your mouth open.	*Nelson Algren*
Time	evaporating like spilled wine – quickly, unnoticed.	*D. H. Lawrence*
Times Law Reports	The further you get, the more they resemble *Alice in Wonderland* crossed with a D'Oyly Carte operetta.	*S. J. Perelman*
Timid	as a titmouse.	*Anon.*
Timid	looks as if the wood were full of thieves.	*Anon.*
Timpani	crunched like candy thunder.	*Anthony Burgess*

Tip	She gave him her nickel with the manner of one presenting a park to a city.	*Dorothy Parker*
Tired	He looks like a piece of chewed twine.	*Anon.*
Tired	We looked like a gang of lost corpses heading back to the boneyard.	*Woody Guthrie*
Together	unavoidably, like two ships becalmed.	*Joseph Conrad*
Tone	as dry as a martini.	*Peter de Vries*
Tongue	wagging like the south end of a goose.	*Anon. (Ozark – USA)*
Tongue	like a lizard's back.	*Raymond Chandler*
Topless bathing	. . . normally shy English breasts bespatter the beach like so many poached eggs.	*Barry Norman*
Torn	like a playground in an earthquake.	*Richard Brautigan*
Touchy	as gunpowder.	*Jilly Cooper*
Tough	as an ingrowing toenail.	*Raymond Chandler*
Traffic	crawled like a wounded snake.	*Ross Macdonald*
Tragedy	. . . not such a tragedy. Like losing a wooden leg in an accident.	*Peter de Vries*

Translations   like wives, are seldom faithful if they are in the least attractive.
Roy Campbell

Trapped   like a trap in a trap.
Dorothy Parker

Tree   . . . the leafless branches look like glass nervous systems in the blue air.
Clive James

Trembling   like a prize essay being read out to the entire school plus the board of governors.
Keith Waterhouse

Tried sorely   like a wolf on the steppes of Russia which has seen its peasant shin up a high tree.
P. G. Wodehouse

Trouble   as much trouble as a loft full of pigeons.
Anon.

Troubled   like a man who has passed through the furnace and been caught in the machinery.
P. G. Wodehouse

Troubles   are like hills. They look impossibly steep from a distance but as we approach them they seem to flatten out before us.
Peter de Vries

Trout   slender as a snake you'd expect to find in a jewellery store.
Richard Brautigan

Trust   no further than I could spit a rat.
Douglas Adams

Trusting   like sending a goat to tend the cabbage.
Anon.

Tubby   . . . a tubby little chap who looked as if he had been poured into his clothes and had forgotten to say 'When'.
P. G. Wodehouse

Turn down   like a bedspread.
Anon.

TV   . . . chewing gum for the eyes.
Frank Lloyd Wright

TV Awards   Getting an award from TV is like getting kissed by someone with bad breath.
Mason Williams

Twitter

like baby starlings welcoming their mother with a worm.
Keith Waterhouse

Ugliness	hangs on me like cheap heavy clothes. *Martin Amis*
Ugly	She was a really bad-looking girl. Facially she resembled Louis Armstrong's voice. *Woody Allen*
Ugly	. . . a face like a bag of spanners. *Anon.*
Ugly	as a starless midnight. *Anon.*
Ugly	look like the back end of a bus. *Anon.*
Ugly	look like the break up of a hard winter. *Anon.*
Ugly	look like a buffalo's bum. *Anon.*
Ugly	so ugly it looks as if she's been beaten with an ugly stick. *Anon.*
Ugly	She's so ugly she has to blindfold the baby before it will suck. *Anon. (Ozark – USA)*
Ugly	like a gargoyle hewn by a drunken stonemason for the adornment of a Methodist Chapel in one of the vilest suburbs of Leeds or Wigan. *Max Beerbohm*
Ugly	. . . a shape like a stone and a face like a baked yam. *Ken Kesey*
Unavailable	as hard to get as a controlling interest in General Motors. *Raymond Chandler*
Uncomfortable	like crossing the Andes in a prison bus. *Hunter S. Thompson*
Uncommunicative	like speaking to a slab of tripe. *Anon.*

Unction	like vaseline with a flavour of port wine. *Aldous Huxley*
Understate	like gazing into the Grand Canyon and remarking, 'Well, well, well; quite a slice.' *Dorothy Parker*
Undress	She took her clothes off like a kite takes gently to a warm April wind. He fumbled his clothes off like a football game being played in November mud. *Richard Brautigan*
Unemotional	and methodical as a country policeman. *David Niven*
Unexpected	as an extra step at the bottom of a flight of stairs. *Jilly Cooper*
Unglazed pottery	looks like the inside of a hen-house. *Victoria Wood*
Unhappy	like a dying duck in a thunderstorm. *Anon.*
Unhappy	like a tragedy queen on one of her bad mornings. *P. G. Wodehouse*
Union militancy	Militancy is like Marmite. A little goes a long way. *Terence Casey*
Unkempt	looking like an accident going somewhere to happen. *Anon.*

Unlikely	like Nixon not knowing about Watergate. *Anon.*

Unlikely	like hearing that Rodgers had decided to sell Hammerstein. *P. G. Wodehouse*
Unobtrusive	as an earthquake. *William McIlvanney*
Unperturbed	as a bank president refusing a loan. *Raymond Chandler*
Unprepossessing	. . . skin like a water-biscuit and legs like two vacuum cleaner bags. *Denis Norden*
Unreal	as Achilles. *Stella Gibbons*
Unreliable	as many faces as a churchyard clock. *Anon.*
Unresponsive	Trying to tell the prime minister anything is like making an important phone call and getting an answering machine. *David Steel*
Unsexy	. . . well-built without being in the slightest bit sexy, like a junior minister's wife. *Denis Norden*
Untidy	looking like the Aeolian stable. *Anon.*
Untidy	like he'd been chewing tobacco and spitting into the wind. *Anon. (Ozark – USA)*
Untidy soldiers	we looked like sacks of shit tied up in the middle. *Spike Milligan*
Unwanted	like a Negro waiter in Rhodesia House, Nashville, Tennessee. *Martin Amis*

Unwanted	like a spare prick at a wedding.	*Anon.*
Up and down	like a fiddler's elbow.	*Anon.*
Urge	like that dark unreasonable urge that impels women to clean house in the middle of the night.	*James Thurber*
Urinate	When he urinated it sounded like the night prayer.	*F. Scott Fitzgerald*
Use	as much use as a button on a hat.	*Anon.*
Use	as much use as a hairnet in a thunderstorm.	*Anon.*
Use	as much use as hay to a goose.	*Anon.*
Use	as much use as an umbrella to a duck.	*Anon.*
Useful	as a chocolate teapot.	*Anon.*
Useful	as a concrete parachute.	*Anon.*
Useful	as a rubber dagger in a knife fight.	*Barry Norman*
Useless	as tits on a boar hog.	*Anon.*
Useless	couldn't organise a piss-up in a brewery.	*Anon.*
Useless	couldn't pour water out of a leaky boat.	*Anon.*
Useless	as pounding sand in a rat-hole.	*Anon. (Ozark – USA)*
Useless	as a general who's afraid to be wrong.	*Raymond Chandler*
Useless	as a cat in a dog fight.	*Ross Macdonald*
Useless	as much use as the Venus de Milo has for a pair of gloves.	*William McIlvanney*

Utter   a sound like an elephant taking its foot out of a mud
             hole in a Burmese teak forest.   *P. G. Wodehouse*

Vain	as a teapot with two spouts.	*Anon.*
Vain	as an Etonian duke.	*G. MacDonald Fraser*
Vanish	like breath off a razor blade.	*P. G. Wodehouse*
Vanish	like a family spectre at the crack of dawn.	*P. G. Wodehouse*
Varicose veins	legs like tights full of snooker balls.	*Ken Dodd*
Vehicle	shaped like a superannuated boot.	*Alida Baxter*
Veins	standing out like Spaghetti Junction.	*Anon.*
Veins	like Danish Blue.	*Victoria Wood*
Velocity	of a demoralised glacier.	*Clive James*
Veneration	. . . was so glutinous that it threatened at times to clog his fountain pen.	*S. J. Perelman*
Venice	In comparison with Venice, Hampton Court maze is a football ground.	*Patrick Campbell*
Venice	is like eating an entire box of chocolate liqueurs at one go.	*Truman Capote*
Verse	Publishing a volume of verse is like dropping a rose petal down the Grand Canyon and waiting for the echo.	*Don Marquis*
Vertical	as noon.	*Roy Campbell*
Vice-presidency	The vice-presidency is sort of like the last cookie on the plate. Everybody insists he won't take it, but somebody always does.	*Bill Vaughan*

Vivacious	as a liberty bodice.	*Victoria Wood*

Voice	His voice took on the quality of a cat snagging brushed nylon.	*Douglas Adams*

Voice	trickled like honey on biscuits.	*Douglas Adams*

Voice	[through a loudspeaker] . . . like that of an ogre at the onset of aphasia.	*Kingsley Amis*

Voice	like a concertina that has been left out in the rain.	*Max Beerbohm*

Voice	His voice thickened as though blood were being stirred into it.	*Anthony Burgess*

Voice	pursued him in anger, like that of a kennelled dog cheated of a walk.	*Anthony Burgess*

Voice	as silky as a burnt crust of toast.	*Raymond Chandler*

Voice	as toneless as a police radio.	*Raymond Chandler*

Voice	had the metallic twang of a banjo string.	*Raymond Chandler*

Voice	husky, like an overworked rooster trying to croon.	*Raymond Chandler*

Voice	like a coyote with bronchitis.	*O. Henry*
Voice	like a six hundred dollar funeral.	*Raymond Chandler*
Voice	like old ivory.	*Raymond Chandler*
Voice	that could have been used for paint remover.	*Raymond Chandler*
Voice	that could have been used to split firewood.	*Raymond Chandler*
Voice	that sounded like Orson Welles with his mouth full of crackers.	*Raymond Chandler*
Voice	tight crackling voice, like someone tiptoeing across a lot of eggshells.	*Raymond Chandler*
Voice	you could have cracked a brazil nut on.	*Raymond Chandler*
Voice	. . . a superb brunette with a contralto voice like hot damp fur.	*Gerald Kersh*
Voice	I heard a large voice, slithering along the wire like warm cottonseed oil.	*Dorothy Parker*
Voice	like a slate pencil.	*Edward B. Sheldon*
Voice	that could have been used to defrost a refrigerator.	*Rex Stout*
Voice	like beer trickling out of a jug.	*P. G. Wodehouse*
Voice	that would have frozen an Eskimo.	*P. G. Wodehouse*
Vulnerable	as open oysters.	*Ross Macdonald*

Vultures   perched like broken umbrellas.   *Graham Greene*

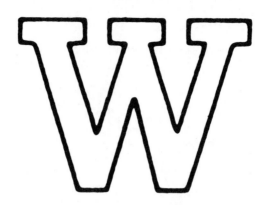

Waiting	like a lamppost.	*R. D. Blackmore*
Waiting	like aeroplane tickets.	*Richard Brautigan*
Walk	like he had gravel in his shoes.	*George Ade*
Walk	like he was belly-deep in cold water.	*Anon. (Ozark – USA)*
Walk away	She churned away like a Nile steamer, with a long brown ripple of Pekingese spaniel in her wake.	*Saki*
Walk softly	as if treading on rose glass with tap shoes.	*Rex Reed*
Wallpaper	like a florist's catalogue.	*Dorothy L. Sayers*
Wan and Wasted	like a summer moon.	*George Mackay Brown*
Wanted	as a Christmas Tree on Twelfth Night.	*Jilly Cooper*
War	is like love; it always finds a way.	*Bertolt Brecht*
Warm	as a mouse in a churn.	*Anon.*
Warm	as a sunned cat.	*Anon.*
Warm	as a posset.	*Anthony Burgess*
Warm	I will warm the sheets like an electric toaster, I will lie by your side like the Sunday roast.	*Dylan Thomas*
Wary	like a fox that had had the Pytchley after it for years.	*P. G. Wodehouse*
Wave	with a hand like a wounded bird. It flutters then drops.	*George Mackay Brown*

Weak	as a lamb that can't stand the weight of its own wool.	
		Anon.

Weak	as a wet dishcloth.	*Anon.*
Weak	so weak he can't fight his way out of a wet paper bag.	
		Anon.
Weak	as a Chinaman's tea.	*Raymond Chandler*
Weak	as a worn-out washer.	*Raymond Chandler*
Weather	uncertain as a baby's butt – you can't tell what's coming.	*Anon. (Ozark – USA)*
Weep	gowking and gobbling like a cow choked on the shaws of a mearns swede.	*Lewis Grassic Gibbon*
Weep	Her face seemed no more than a breaking dyke that could barely hold back the snot and phlegm that shifted behind it.	*William McIlvanney*
Welcome	as Attila the Hun.	*Anon.*
Welcome	as a bacon sandwich at a bar mitzvah.	*Anon.*
Welcome	as a flea in the bed.	*Anon.*

Welcome	as a plague of locusts.	*Anon.*
Welcome	as water in a leaking shoe.	*Anon.*
Welcome	as if he was the much-loved family dog who had gone missing for three weeks.	*Tom Davies*
Welcome	as a polecat at a picnic.	*Charles Henderson*
Welcome	as an earwig in one's meringue.	*Patrick Moore*
Welcome	as a boil on the cheekbone.	*P. G. Wodehouse*
Well-behaved	as a mouse in a jar of nut crunch.	*Rachel Mackie*
Well-endowed	built like a brick shit-house.	*Anon.*
Well-endowed	stacked like a timber yard.	*Anon.*
Well-groomed	as a cat.	*Anon.*
Well-preserved	like blackcurrant jam.	*Anon.*
Wet	enough to bog a duck.	*Anon. (Australia)*
Wet	as mother's dish-clouts.	*John Buchan*
Wet	as any catfish in any creek ever was or ever will be.	*Woody Guthrie*
Wheeze	like a man who has just won a pie eating contest.	*Raymond Chandler*
Wheeze	like a furred-up steam kettle.	*John McVicar*
Whiskers	. . . of a Victorian bushiness and give the impression of having been grown under glass.	*P. G. Wodehouse*

Whisper	a compressed whisper that made her words reach me like a kind of lethal gas.	*Peter de Vries*
White	as a whitewashed crow.	*Anon.*
White	as an angel's ass.	*Peter Benchley*
Whiter	than an angel's wing.	*Raymond Chandler*
Wide-eyed	as a marigold.	*Dorothy Parker*
Wild	as a marshtigget in May.	*Stella Gibbons*
Wilder	than a woodchuck.	*Woody Guthrie*
Wimbledon trophy	looks disconcertingly like a digestive biscuit.	*Ronald Atkin*
Wine	tasted like a wet sheepdog.	*Anon.*
Wink	as casual as lowering and raising a flag.	*William McIlvanney*
Wink	like a heliograph.	*Sir Compton Mackenzie*
Wise	as a brace of owls.	*Roger McGough*
Wiser	than a treeful of owls.	*Damon Runyon*
Wit	like a hummingbird's beak.	*Anon.*
Withdrawn	so withdrawn you would have had to sink a mine to get to him.	*William McIlvanney*
Wobbled	like an old lady with too many parcels.	*Raymond Chandler*
Woman	Twenty years of romance make a woman look like a ruin; but twenty years of marriage make her something like a public building.	*Oscar Wilde*
Women	are like lobsters; the tenderest meat is in the claws.	*Peter de Vries*

Woods   which smelled like a warm oven.   *Leslie Thomas*

Words   kept falling like dead leaves from his mouth.
                                                     William McIlvanney

Words   fell like the thud of clods on a coffin-lid.
                                                     Dorothy Parker

Words   fashioned with a somewhat overprecise diction, like
                     shapes turned out by a cookie cutter.   *Peter de Vries*

Work at home   My children hop like fleas in a box . . . and I work
                     among cries and clatters like a venomous beaver in a
                     parrot house.   *Dylan Thomas*

Worry   as much as dandruff would a chopped-off head.
                                                     William McIlvanney

Wound   beating like an auxiliary heart.   *Ross Macdonald*

Wrinkled   as Methuselah on his 969th birthday.   *Cass McCallum*

Wrinkled   radiating wrinkles like an apprentice Michelin Man.
                                                     William McIlvanney

Write   he makes all other dramatic commentators . . . look as
                   if they spelled out their reviews with alphabet blocks.
                                        Dorothy Parker (of George Jean Nathan)

Writer   As he says, he has a way with words; as Crippen had
                   with wives.   *Cliff Hanley*

Writhe   like an electric fan.   *P. G. Wodehouse*

Writing   Sometimes I think it sounds like I walked out of the
                   room and left the typewriter running.   *Gene Fowler*

Wrong   as Prohibition.   *Dashiell Hammett*

Wronged   feeling like Romeo if Juliet had shoved him off the
                   balcony and then laughed like stink at his fractured
                   leg.   *Richard Gordon*

Yellow   as a canary lacking in moral fibre.   *Anon.*

Young actress   who leaps about the stage with all the abandon of a
                    young doe being pursued by an elderly banker.
                                                        Groucho Marx

Young and   looks like his teeth will stay in all night.   *Victoria Wood*
handsome

SPARE